A Project Sponsor's Warp-Speed Guide

A Project Sponsor's Warp-Speed Guide

Improving Project Performance

Yogi Schulz, B. Comm, and Jocelyn Schulz Lapointe, MPA, PMP

BEP

BUSINESS EXPERT PRESS

Leader in applied, concise business books

We dedicate this book to the Schulz family. For decades, they've had to put up with many project management discussions across the dinner table. They are also the leading characters for many of the anecdotes in the sidebars throughout this book.

We also dedicate this book to Trevor Lapointe, Jocelyn's husband, who provided countless hours of child management on evenings and weekends so Jocelyn could write this book. He finally admitted after 12 years of marriage to a project manager, that he doesn't like the term "critical path."

Description

Are you new to the project sponsor role or want to improve? This book's *practical guidance* will help you successfully fulfill your role. We understand you are time-challenged. This book is *short, direct,* and focuses on the most common project issues. The book's guidance is helpful for projects of all sizes and across all sectors. The fundamental questions apply to projects from strip mining to large public works projects and even your weekend warrior home renovation projects. We think that Tolstoy would agree that all happy projects are alike, while unhappy projects are unhappy in their unique ways.

We begin the book with a brief assessment to help you understand your project's risks. You can complete the *warp-speed project assessment* in a few minutes. By completing the assessment, you will understand the topics that need more attention to reduce the project's shortcomings and increase its likelihood of success. We recommend practical actions you can champion to position the project for success for each topic.

The book describes the most common project topics that can contribute to either project success or failure. The topics cover a wide range of situations. The suggested actions can be scaled down easily and adapted for smaller projects.

Completing the *warp-speed project assessment* will assess your project's risks and better understand the topics that need more attention. With our *practical actions,* you can champion the project for *success.*

We've grouped the topics into the typical project phases found in *A Guide to the Project Management Body of Knowledge* (PMBOK Guide), published by the Project Management Institute (PMI). We also use the PMBOK terminology throughout the book and provide cross-references to the PMBOK Guide. These book features will facilitate your communication with your team because it is often familiar with the PMBOK Guide.

Keywords

project sponsor; project; project management; project risk; project assessment; *A Guide to the Project Management Body of Knowledge*; PMBOK Guide; Project Management Institute; PMI

Contents

Testimonials

"Seeing Yogi Schulz and Jocelyn Schulz Lapointe tackle an ignored topic is gratifying. Typically, project sponsors receive too little orientation for their role. Written in an accessible style using clear, straightforward language, this guide will help many project sponsors improve the value they can bring to projects." **—Robin Hornby, Senior Project Consultant, Author of *Commercial Project Management***

"Senior executives are often responsible for projects that are critically important to their organization's strategic initiatives. Many are often unsure how they can be effective project sponsors to ensure the success of these critical projects. The book's contents, organization, and practical tips will enable any project sponsor to quickly understand their role and how they can add value to ensure successful projects." **—Ron Murch Senior Instructor Emeritus, University of Calgary, Haskayne School of Business**

"The warp-speed *guide offers many practical, real-world examples and references that project sponsors and project managers will find extremely useful."* **—Jim Boyes, Operations and Program Manager, Industry Sandbox and AI Computing (ISAIC)**

"I immediately related the book's content to my role as a project sponsor for various AWS consulting projects." **—Dave Jackson, National Healthcare Lead—Canada, AWS Profession Services**

Foreword

In my professional work as a consultant, project manager, and leadership coach, I have observed many project sponsors. Their performance varies all over the map, from helpful and supportive to downright dysfunctional and counterproductive.

Many of the project sponsors I have encountered would benefit from using this book as a reference guide, even if they didn't take the time to read it in its entirety. Project managers can also benefit from this book by ensuring they've covered the book's topics.

This book tackles the most common project issues that should make project sponsors nervous. These issues, such as the project sponsor/project manager relationship, repeatedly arise during my work as a project management leadership coach. The book provides practical, tactical actions that project sponsors can take, typically collaborating with their project manager, to position their project for success.

This book starts with a unique project assessment that can help time-challenged executives typically, acting as project sponsors, focus a vague, nagging feeling into specific observations that can be addressed to mitigate project risks.

I have known Yogi Schulz professionally for over 20 years. We first met when he offered to present at a ProjectWorld conference that my company produced. Yogi continued to present on various topics at my conferences in several Canadian cities for many years.

While I haven't met his daughter and coauthor Jocelyn Lapointe, I'm sure Yogi taught her the core principles of project management from birth. Jocelyn provides a more modern and youthful take on project management in this book, relying on her expertise as a health care project manager.

A father–daughter duo in project management is rare, but these two have written a compelling book. They've peppered lots of fun homespun anecdotes throughout this book to make it easily relatable.

Yogi has coached many project sponsors as an experienced consultant and project manager. While that's never part of the published job description, coaching the project sponsor can be a critical success factor for completing projects successfully. This book contains his recommendations to project sponsors and managers based on those many years of experience.

Yogi's perspective on project management best practices was always well received by the attendees of my project management conferences.

Yogi Schulz has led many information technology projects to a successful conclusion as a project manager. In a few cases, he's rescued looming disasters. This book contains his recommendations to project sponsors based on the issues that arose during those projects.

Yogi Schulz has developed and delivered seminars and conference presentations on various project management topics.

Recently Yogi Schulz contributed multiple videos to my ProjectBites website. Two of the videos touch on the topics discussed in the book.

As a project sponsor or a project manager, you will find many good ideas for increasing the likelihood of project success in this book.

—David Barrett
(Creating and curating content for project managers,
business analysts and project leaders)
Author of the regular video series on Leadership Perspectives
Producer of the ProjectBites videos website
President, Solutions Network Inc., Toronto, Ontario

Preface

We have learned from our experience as project managers that time-challenged executives need a short, practical book to help them fulfill the project sponsor role. We chose warp-speed for the title because we wanted these executives to know immediately that we're responding to the realities of their time-pressured lives. Our book contains short discussions of projects' many topics and focuses on practical actions that position projects for success. This book is not another giant, difficult-to-read, exhaustive, and exhausting academic dissertation on project management.

Too often, we've observed that these project sponsors:

1. Do not understand this role
2. Are unsure about what others expect
3. Have little or no direct experience with the project subject and mistakenly assume that such a background is essential
4. Are too embarrassed to ask for help
5. Receive no guidance from their organization

As a result, project sponsors too often retreat into a cursory figurehead role or ignore the role to the detriment of the project.

To help project sponsors succeed, we begin the book with a warp-speed project assessment about common project topics to assess the project's issues. Because we know how time-challenged executives are, we designed the assessment so anyone can complete it in a few minutes. Completing the assessment requires no specific expertise. By completing the assessment, sponsors will understand the topics that need more attention to reduce their project's risks and increase its likelihood of success. We describe practical actions that sponsors can champion to position the project for success for each topic.

We explain the most common project topics that can contribute to either project success or failure. For each topic, we provide two brief descriptions to help project sponsors determine if the topic needs more attention or not. We offer a short description of the recommended actions for every topic, leading to reduced risk and a higher likelihood of project success.

Executives often don't understand how valuable performing this project sponsor role can be to:

1. Reduce project risk
2. Avoid embarrassing project failure
3. Contribute to achieving the benefit the organization hopes to gain from their investment in the project

Acknowledgments

We are grateful to Kam Jugdev and Tim Kloppenborg for suggesting we undertake writing this book and providing their editorial comments. The team at Business Expert Press has been invaluable in coaching us through editing the manuscript, preparing the manuscript for publication, and defining the marketing plan.

We acknowledge Robin Hornby, who provided invaluable feedback on the draft manuscript. Robin is a career project manager who has interacted with many project sponsors who exhibited a wide range of interest and engagement in the project Robin managed.

We also appreciate Thibault Dambrine, Dave Jackson, Ron Murch, Mark Perrin, and Gary Silberg, who provided helpful feedback on the draft manuscript.

CHAPTER 1

Executive Summary

Yogi and Jocelyn wrote this book for you, the project sponsor, because we've observed projects flounder firsthand when the project sponsor is absent or unsure of their role. As project managers, we've suffered dysfunctional consequences when project sponsors do not fulfill their roles.

We chose warp-speed[1] for the title in recognition of the time constraints that are the reality of the lives of most executives. Completing the following warp-speed project assessment and taking action where needed will help you:

1. Reduce the risk of a disappointing project outcome.
2. Identify areas where your intervention is critical to project success.
3. Support your project manager and the team better.
4. Fulfill your role as project sponsor[2] more effectively.

You know you *should* know the status and risks of your project, but you don't really *feel* like you do. You want your project to succeed. Your business depends on it. You don't want project failure to damage your carefully nurtured reputation, your organization's standing in the community, or its well-regarded brand. You also don't want others in the organization to view your project as a boondoggle or a career-killing project.

As the project sponsor, you've listened to some presentations, seen some spreadsheets, received status reports, and discussed the project with your project manager. However, you aren't confident that your project is progressing as expected. Your nagging feeling is telling you that something definitely isn't right.

To help you translate your vague, nagging feeling into a specific observation that you can act on to mitigate project issues, we designed

---

[1] See the Glossary entry for Warp-speed.
[2] See Appendix A—Role of Project Sponsors for more detail.

the assessment to be quick and straightforward to complete. Completing it will reveal what topic is causing your nagging feeling of unease. As you read through the contrasting observations in the assessment, note which ones ring true to you. Then, implement the suggested actions for responding to the high-risk observation. We believe this warp-speed approach will focus your limited time on actions that will contribute the most to project success.

This book describes many observations that frequently occur in all projects. We've selected topics that are the most common sources of project success or failure. We've arranged these topics by their related PMBOK Guide[3] project phase.[4]

Earlier project phases contain more topics than later phases. This emphasis reflects the reality that the many decisions agreed to, not recognized as necessary or dodged during the initial phases, position projects for later success or failure. Evaluate your observations regardless of the current phase of your project. For example, even though your project is in the deploy phase, the root cause of your observation may have occurred much earlier in the planning phase.

In the history of humankind, no one has ever said: "This project has turned out to be easier than I thought at the beginning." Every project encounters unanticipated issues. The project sponsor collaborates with the project manager[5] and stakeholders to mitigate the impact of those issues as the project proceeds.

---

[3] *A Guide to the Project Management Body of Knowledge* (PMBOK Guide), published by the Project Management Institute. We deliberately chose the project phases described in the PMBOK Guide as the framework for this book because it aligns the book with the universal language of project managers.

[4] See the Glossary entry for Phase.

[5] The project sponsor and project manager function in distinct roles. The project sponsor does not ignore, intimidate, back-seat drive or micromanage the project manager. The project manager does not manipulate the project sponsor.

CHAPTER 2

Introduction

We've written this book to help you, a busy project sponsor, fulfill your role, support your team's work, and be time-efficient. It's based on the numerous frustrations we've experienced when project sponsors haven't been oriented for their role. Don't feel bad! Many organizations are terrible at project sponsor orientation. We are still waiting to find an organization that does this well. Most people think any executive, vice president, or manager is experienced enough to be a great project sponsor without orientation. This assumption is not accurate. But with the tips and tricks in this book, you can develop this critical skill and keep your project on track.

By reading relevant topics in the book, you can become more effective as a project sponsor and increase the likelihood of success for your project. You have the power to make a difference.

The book emphasizes ongoing collaboration between the project sponsor and the project manager. It also recognizes that their roles and responsibilities differ. The roles and, by implication, the differences are described in the first few appendices at this link: www.jocelynlapointe .com/resources.

This book is not intended to be a comprehensive guide to all parts of the role of a project sponsor. It focuses only on topics that frequently derail projects and describes how you can intervene to ensure the success of your project.

You don't need to read much of this book to derive value from it. After completing the warp-speed project assessment, treat the book more like a reference book and read just the page about the topic of immediate concern. Each topic in the book stands independently of all others.

Effective Project Sponsors Fulfill Their Role

Your role as a project sponsor includes the following major elements:[1]

1. Accountable for project business results
2. Provides project budget
3. Champions project benefits throughout the organization
4. Provides support and guidance for the project manager
5. Provides support and encouragement to the team
6. Ensures resource commitments are fulfilled
7. Resolves issues that the project manager cannot resolve on their own
8. Needs no technical expertise or experience related to the project deliverables

Figure 2.1 Project sponsors sometimes don't take their role seriously

See the Glossary for the definition of PMO.

First and foremost, project sponsors provide funding for the project and expect its estimated benefits will be delivered. Please read Appendix A—Role of Project Sponsors for a more detailed discussion of the project sponsor's role.

Determined Project Sponsors Take Action

You are an experienced executive who is comfortable making decisions routinely. Decisions typically require judgment because they are frequently made with incomplete information. Similarly, your role as a project sponsor involves judgment. We've observed that project sponsors

---

[1] Please read Appendix A—Role of Project Sponsors for more detail on these points.

are often too cautious in making judgments because they are unfamiliar with the details of the project. Being too careful or hesitant lets problems fester, grow, and become more significant to the detriment of project success. Indecision is more detrimental to project success than decisions that turn out wrong later.[2] This counterintuitive statement is true because adding elapsed time to project schedules adds cost and risk.

We encourage you to take determined action[3] in consultation with the project manager to mitigate the impact of high-risk situations. We've provided many suggested actions throughout the book. Through action and encouraging action, you can position your project for success. Action is always better than hoping for the best.

Conversely, if you're being sucked into too many issues that you think should be handled by the project manager or the team, please read Appendix B—What Project Sponsors Don't Do.

How to Use This Book

Here is a list of ways this book can help you depending on your immediate situation:

1. Use this book as a reference guide as your project progresses if you don't have the time to read it entirely.
2. Use the table of contents to hone in on the topics that will be of immediate interest for your current project phase.
3. Use the index to identify just the topic of interest that is creating that gnawing feeling of doubt now.
4. Flip through the book to read actions that address various topics that may concern you.
5. Skim a PDF copy of the warp-speed project assessment at this in the Resources section of the book's website (www.jocelynlapointe.com/resources) to help you narrow in on the topic creating that gnawing feeling of doubt.

---

[2] Decisions may turn out later to be not quite right. Nonetheless, decisions provide immediate direction and will raise understanding and clarity of project issues and opportunities. Indecision does not advance understanding.

[3] See the Glossary entry for Bias for action.

Demonstrating Decisiveness When Stranded in Manhattan

Your authors, Yogi, Jocelyn, and Yogi's wife, Connie, became unexpectedly stranded in New York during a sudden winter snowstorm. Jocelyn and her family had moved to New Jersey only four months earlier and were now proudly showing Yogi and Connie Manhattan when a sudden snowstorm hit. All the roads, buses, trains, and boats out of the city were rapidly stalled by gridlock and then canceled. We needed to return to Jocelyn's home soon. Jocelyn took Connie and Yogi to Penn station, hoping to find a train home. When they arrived, it was mass hysteria. Everyone in Manhattan seemed to be pursuing the same goal as your authors. There was no direction and no hope. There were multiple ways out of the city to Jocelyn's home in NJ, but, as a newcomer, she wasn't familiar with them and could not determine the best, given the wintery conditions. Fortunately, Connie noticed a half-full train that purported to go to a nearby New Jersey station. Not the perfect station but close to Jocelyn's house. At least it was a way to leave the city. Connie convinced Yogi and Jocelyn to board the train. It was the last train leaving Penn Station that day and was packed with many anxious passengers. We made it to New Jersey and walked to Jocelyn's apartment through the ankle-deep snow. Everyone was tired and cold but grateful for Connie's decisive action to jump on that train.

Project sponsors must be decisive in unknown or ambiguous circumstances like Connie. Dithering[4] on decisions will mean your project will miss the metaphorical train and wind up stranded on Manhattan's snowy, gridlocked streets.

Figure 2.2 Navigating a Manhattan snowstorm

---

[4] See the Glossary entry for Bias for action.

CHAPTER 3

Warp-Speed Project Assessment Introduction

Please read and complete the warp-speed project assessment in the next chapter. We've designed it specifically for the project sponsor's perspective.

You can download and complete additional PDF copies of the project assessment at this link: www.jocelynlapointe.com/resources.

Value of the Warp-Speed Project Assessment

Many topics we discuss in this book can derail projects. Analysis of successful and failed projects reveals that the topics listed as follows in the project assessment frequently contribute to either project success or failure.

Completing the assessment provides a way to bring that gnawing feeling of doubt about your project into the open, with little effort, in a constructive way. We've selected the topics to help you quickly uncover the specific difficulty your project may be experiencing.

Simply sharing your gnawing feeling of doubt with the project manager, or worse, the team without factual evidence, will only undermine the confidence the team needs to feel in you and your commitment to the project.

In addition to the assessment, the Management By Wandering Around (MBWA) technique provides another way to better focus on that gnawing feeling of doubt.

How to Complete the Warp-Speed Project Assessment

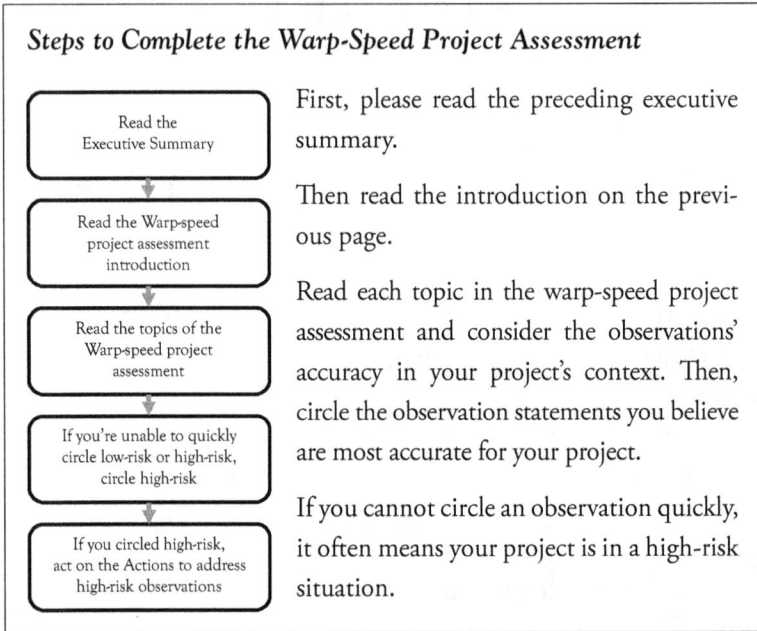

Steps to Complete the Warp-Speed Project Assessment

Read the Executive Summary
↓
Read the Warp-speed project assessment introduction
↓
Read the topics of the Warp-speed project assessment
↓
If you're unable to quickly circle low-risk or high-risk, circle high-risk
↓
If you circled high-risk, act on the Actions to address high-risk observations

First, please read the preceding executive summary.

Then read the introduction on the previous page.

Read each topic in the warp-speed project assessment and consider the observations' accuracy in your project's context. Then, circle the observation statements you believe are most accurate for your project.

If you cannot circle an observation quickly, it often means your project is in a high-risk situation.

Figure 3.1 Completing the warp-speed project assessment

For a more extensive description of each topic, please read the related section shown below each topic.[1] If you're unsure which observations are accurate for your project, you are not close enough to the project and need to allocate a little more time to fulfill your role as a project sponsor.

Once you've answered the questions, read the sections applicable to the topics where you circled observations in the high-risk box. These sections will help you determine what actions to take next to explore solutions to your high-risk observation.

Then decide which high-risk topics you will discuss with your project manager. The conversation concerns assigning the actions you and the project manager will take to reduce project risk and your gnawing

---

[1] We've grouped the topics by the project phases used in the PMBOK Guide. For each topic, we've also provided a cross-reference to the applicable section of the PMBOK Guide if you want to learn more about the topic.

feeling of doubt about the project. This conversation needs to be collaborative. It is not helpful to approach your project manager by waving the assessment and accusing them of mismanaging the project based on your answers.

It may be helpful to complete the project assessment with your project manager. That will allow you to develop your working relationship as you share observations. You can then collaborate on specific actions to reduce project risks and improve performance. Similarly, reviewing your answers with your project manager can effectively build your relationship and allow you to share your concerns in a supportive manner.

CHAPTER 4

Warp-Speed Project Assessment

We recommend completing the assessment in its entirety before you take any action. You may already know exactly where your problem lies and want to read the topic specifically devoted to this problem. While this might seem like a faster way to solve your immediate issue, the root cause of the problem you are currently experiencing might have occurred earlier in the project. You may miss the root cause of your problem by not completing the assessment in its entirety. Many issues that arise when deploying stem from improperly executing the planning or design phase. Proceed at your own risk.

Feasibility

Topic	Low-risk observations	High-risk observations
Project sponsor	I am the senior executive appointed to the role of the project sponsor. I'm confident in my ability to fulfill the position.	No one has been appointed the project sponsor. Multiple individuals share the position. The president is the project sponsor.
Project manager	A full-time project manager, who has my confidence, is in place. The project manager has the appropriate experience.	The project manager has other competing responsibilities. Multiple individuals share the project management role.
Project business case	There is a document that describes the project's business case. The data underlying the business case makes sense to me. I can summarize the business case as an elevator pitch.	There is no documented business case. The business case data is overly optimistic, or the business case is just a narrative. I can't summarize the business case succinctly.

(Continues)

(*Continued*)

Topic	Low-risk observations	High-risk observations
Project goal	I've seen a crisp, sensible, one-sentence statement of the project goal.	The project goal statement is a long paragraph. I've heard a lot of debate about goals and various conflicting statements.
Project objectives	I've seen short statements of project objectives. The project objectives support the project goal.	I've heard a lot of debates about objectives and various conflicting statements. I've heard no discussion about project objectives.
Scope statements	A comprehensive set of scope statements exist. The scope statements clearly state what is in-scope and out-of-scope for this project.	There is no scope statement. The scope statements are vague and incomplete. My team is unclear about what is in and out of this project's scope.
Project charter	I've seen a reasonably comprehensive project charter.	The project charter I've seen is vague and incomplete. No project charter has been prepared.
Project benefits	I can articulate the project benefits. I view the estimates of tangible benefits as reasonable.	I observe varying perceptions about the reality of project benefits. No one has had time to estimate benefits. Most of the benefits are intangible.
Project budget	I've seen the budget, and the principal line-item amounts look reasonable.	I've not reviewed or approved a project budget. The budget line-item amounts change over time. The budget I've seen shows a much lower total dollar amount than I expected.

Planning

Topic	Low-risk observations	High-risk observations
Project management plan	I've reviewed the project management plan, which looks complete.	I've not seen a project management plan. The project management plan feels incomplete or vague, or ambiguous. Various documents contain different parts of the project management plan.

Topic	Low-risk observations	High-risk observations
Project sponsor/ project manager relationship	The project manager and I understand one another's work styles. I am consulted on important issues that the team is facing at suitable intervals. The project manager and I communicate in person or over video chat regularly. I am comfortable initiating informal discussions with the project manager to keep myself well-informed.	The project manager and I experience constant misunderstandings. I am consulted too much or too little about issues related to the project. The project manager and I communicate infrequently. Informal discussions with the project manager are rare and feel awkward.
Project resources	The team members I've met appear to have the requisite skills and experience. The team has acquired or contracted other resources.	Multiple individuals on the team I've met appear not to have sufficient skills and experience or exhibit a good work ethic. The team has not acquired or only partially contracted for other resources.
Team organization	I've seen a reasonably clear organization chart with mostly full-time employees and only a few empty boxes.	I've seen an organization chart with too many contractors, multiple empty boxes, or too many lines.
Project technology	The team consistently uses a shortlist of technologies. I can conceptually describe the technologies.	The team uses an extensive and changing list of technologies. New technology buzzwords abound in discussions.
Project schedule	I've seen a comprehensive project schedule visualized as a Gantt chart. The schedule is available and understood by the team.	I haven't seen a comprehensive project schedule. The team doesn't appear to understand the project schedule. The Gantt chart of the project schedule changes materially from one report to the next.
Effort estimates	I've seen effort estimates for tasks and believe them to be reasonable.	I've not seen many effort estimates for tasks. I'm concerned that available estimates tend to be duration estimates.
Risk identification	I've observed that the team has identified potential risks in a risk register. The work looks comprehensive to me.	I've not observed the team performing risk identification. The risk register looks incomplete to me.

(Continues)

(*Continued*)

Topic	Low-risk observations	High-risk observations
Project steering committee	The key business areas that will be affected by the project are represented. The committee meets every 4 to 6 weeks.	I don't know if a steering committee exists. Membership is unclear. Meetings are sporadic or offer little content.
Project consensus	Project team members, departments directly involved, and other stakeholders have agreed to the goal and objectives.	Whenever I speak to team members, departments directly involved, and other stakeholders, I hear substantial variations on the goal and objectives.
Long lead-time items	I've seen a list of long lead-time items. I'm aware of the dialogue between the team and a few potential vendors, even though a detailed design is not ready.	I've not seen a list of long lead-time items. The team knows that some long lead-time items will be required but has not taken specific planning action.
Physical space	My team occupies a suitable physical space to conduct the project. My team has the needed desks, offices, computers, phones, and conference rooms. They have the space to store project materials when necessary.	My team is scattered throughout the building, even though working in proximity would be most efficient. Team members complain that they squeeze into a small conference room that they can only book sometimes. Insufficient warehouse space is creating logistics problems.

Design

Topic	Low-risk observations	High-risk observations
Project requirements	I've seen a detailed report of functional and nonfunctional requirements.	The report of project requirements I've seen is too high level or uneven in detail. The team has not achieved a consensus on the requirements. The report of project requirements is incredibly detailed and sounds more like a design document.

Topic	Low-risk observations	High-risk observations
Client engagement	The client consistently provides the necessary resources, such as business staff and systems, to make the project successful.	I'm aware that the team can't access the resources required to make the project successful, such as business staff, login credentials, and company policies.
Internal politics	I've heard stakeholders make supportive comments about the project. When I enlisted the help of stakeholders, they completed the agreed actions.	I've heard stakeholders make critical comments about the project. I've heard derisive comments about the project manager and individual team members. When I enlisted the help of stakeholders, they listened politely but didn't agree to take action.
Stakeholder engagement	I know that affected stakeholders know our project is actively underway. I've seen a list of the affected stakeholder groups with the current contact.	I'm aware that affected stakeholders don't know who the project manager is or that a project affecting their work is underway. The list of the affected stakeholder groups is incomplete.
Risk monitoring	I know that the team reviews project risks and regularly updates related mitigations.	I am aware that the team reviews project risks rarely or never.
Product and service procurement	I'm aware of a reasonably rigorous process for procuring products and services.	I'm aware of an arduous and excessively rigorous process for procuring products and services. I've observed that the team procures products and services based on personal relationships.
Vendor contracting	I'm aware of a reasonably structured process for contracting with vendors.	I'm aware of a horrendously complex process for contracting with vendors that consumes significant team effort.
Vendor performance	I've seen information about the vendors' timeliness and quality of deliverables that I assess as acceptable.	I've seen information about the unacceptable quality of the vendor deliverables. I've not seen information about the quality of the vendor deliverables.
Meeting management	I've seen project meeting agendas. I can find the meeting minutes.	I haven't seen meeting agendas. I can't find minutes from previous meetings, or the minutes are incomplete.

(Continues)

Build

Topic	Low-risk observations	High-risk observations
Product design	I've seen complete detailed designs for the project deliverables.	The designs I've seen are too high level or uneven in detail. The team has not achieved a consensus on the design of some deliverables.
Project change management	I've seen a significant list of possible scope additions. But they remain on the list and have not been adopted into the project scope. The project manager rarely recommends scope changes to the project steering committee and me.	I've seen the project manager frequently discuss good ideas that the team adds to the project scope. On multiple occasions, the project manager has recommended scope changes to the project steering committee and me.
Team allocation	I've seen the team assignments to tasks and believe them reasonable.	I've not seen the team assignments to tasks. I'm concerned that some team members are overallocated and some are underallocated.
Project progress	On multiple occasions, I've seen the same summary Gantt chart illustrating reasonable project progress. I've seen metrics such as percent complete, effort-to-date or effort remaining to know which deliverables are underway. Deliverables are completed on time more often than not.	I've never seen a Gantt chart. Successive Gantt charts show little or no progress. I'm simply *hoping* to see a completed deliverable by the due date. I've not seen metrics. Deliverables are often late. My team feels frazzled.
Percent complete	Percent complete is one of multiple metrics reported to me and used to determine that my project is on schedule.	I observe percent complete is often optimistically overstated. Percent complete is the only metric reported to me to determine if my project is on schedule.
Risk mitigation	I've seen risk mitigation tasks that appear comprehensive. I've observed the team performing risk mitigation tasks.	I've not seen the team planning risk mitigation tasks. The team is not performing risk mitigation tasks.

Topic	Low-risk observations	High-risk observations
Project milestones	The project schedule includes essential milestones. The milestone dates I've seen seem realistic and are met more often than not.	The project schedule includes a few milestones. The milestone dates I've seen are often padded, infrequently met, or unknown to the team.
Project communication	I've seen a communication plan. I know who is responsible for project communication with stakeholders and team members. I've seen well-designed communication artifacts. I've seen communication occurring.	I haven't seen a communication plan. I don't know who is responsible for project communication. Communication happens ad hoc and typically in response to stakeholder requests for a status update. Communication artifacts contain contradictory information.
Project expenditures	I receive regular updates on project expenditures. The cumulative expenditure amounts by line item seem plausible to me.	I rarely receive updates on project expenditures. The cumulative expenditure amounts by line item I see vary significantly over time.
Project expenditure forecast	I receive regular project expenditure forecasts. The expenditure forecast amounts by line item seem plausible to me.	I don't receive expenditure forecasts. The expenditure forecast amounts I see vary considerably from one reporting period to the next.
Team environment	I've observed the team interacting respectfully and collaborating well.	I've observed tensions in team conversations. I've observed the project manager treating some team members better than others. I've observed conflict and arguments among team members.

Test

Topic	Low-risk observations	High-risk observations
Acceptance criteria	I've seen a reasonable list of essential criteria that must be met to ensure deliverable acceptance. Most of the acceptance criteria include numeric values.	Various descriptions with no numeric criteria define the deliverable acceptance criteria I've seen. Deliverable acceptance is based on someone's gut feeling. Deliverable acceptance is based on the opinion of the person assigned to complete the deliverable.

(*Continues*)

(*Continued*)

Topic	Low-risk observations	High-risk observations
Quality control (QC)	I've seen a satisfactory quality control plan for the project. I've seen evidence of QC work.	I'm not aware of any QC plan for the project. I haven't seen evidence of QC work.
Quality assurance (QA)	I've seen a suitable QA plan for the project. I've seen QA reports for our project deliverables.	I'm not aware of any QA plan for the project. I haven't seen QA reports for our project deliverables. The QA reports I've seen for our project deliverables appeared incomplete.
Team turnover	Team turnover is low. The team appears happy to be on the project.	Team turnover is surprisingly high. Project morale varies significantly over time.

Deploy

Topic	Low-risk observations	High-risk observations
People change management	The project management plan I've seen includes tasks for people change management. Related work is evident.	I haven't seen people change management referenced in the project management plan. People change management work is informal and sporadic. Related work is not evident.
Data quality	I've seen a data quality evaluation plan, and it's being followed. I've observed data quality improvement work. The supporting data quality standards document looks reasonable.	I've not observed data quality evaluation work. The data quality evaluation I've observed appears rushed and uneven to meet project milestones. I've observed no data quality improvement work. The data quality standards document doesn't exist or looks incomplete.
Operations plan	I've seen an operations plan that looks reasonably complete.	I've not seen an operations plan. The operations plan that I've seen is incomplete.

Close

Topic	Low-risk observations	High-risk observations
Project acceptance	I know who is responsible for accepting the project as complete. *It's very likely you!*	I don't know who is responsible for accepting the project as complete. I can identify multiple people responsible for accepting the project as complete.
Lessons learned	I've reviewed lessons learned being created by my team and believe they will be helpful for subsequent projects. I've reviewed lessons learned from previous projects.	I haven't seen a lessons learned register. We've faced similar issues in other projects but can't remember how they were handled or those solutions' outcomes. The lessons learned register looks incomplete.

You can download and complete additional PDF copies of the project assessment at this link: www.jocelynlapointe.com/resources.

The balance of the book expands on all the topics you've just assessed. Most importantly, we describe actions to address the high-risk observations. At a minimum, completing these actions will reduce project risk. Typically, completing these actions positions the project for successful completion.

CHAPTER 5

Feasibility

Overview

Feasibility is the first project phase. It determines if the business case is valid and if the organization can deliver the intended outcome by describing the project in the charter document.

Don't feel bad about not starting or quickly closing a project that is not feasible or viable. Don't waste resources attempting or continuing a project if you aren't sure of its value. You can position a cancelation as avoiding waste. Don't allow others to spin early cancelation as a failure.

Performing an Adequate Project Feasibility

The construction of the John Hancock Tower in Boston, Massachusetts, encountered multiple engineering problems, including the following:

1. A bungled excavation damaged the nearby Trinity Church.
2. Windows weighing 500 pounds each popped out of the building during high winds. The problem was a design flaw, so all 10,334 panes of glass had to be replaced.
3. The tower swayed in the wind to a dangerous degree. The solution required interior reinforcing to prevent walls and partitions from cracking in high winds.

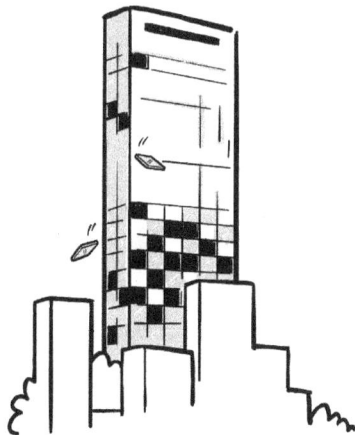

(Continues)

(Continued)

> The problems delayed the building opening from 1971 to 1976 and increased the cost from U.S.$75 million to U.S.$175 million.
>
> You have to wonder how well the engineers and architects conducted the project's feasibility.

Figure 5.1 Engineering problems at the John Hancock Tower

Has a Senior Project Sponsor Been Appointed?

As a project sponsor, you are responsible for management oversight of the project. In addition, you are the link between the project to senior management and business stakeholders that keeps everyone informed and aligned.

Topic	Low-risk observations	High-risk observations
Project sponsor	I am the senior executive appointed to the role of the project sponsor. I'm confident in my ability to fulfill the position.	No one has been appointed the project sponsor. Multiple individuals share the position. The president is the project sponsor.
PMBOK references[1]	Sixth edition: 3.3.3, 3.5	Seventh edition: Appendix X2

Low-Risk Description

I am the project sponsor. Although the project manager reports to me, I respond to the project manager and the team to answer high-level questions about the project's characteristics and expectations. I am a full-time employee with a broad perspective and understanding of the organization. I have worked in multiple areas of the organization. My position is high enough on the organization chart to command action.

---

[1] For every topic, we've provided references to more related information in the PMBOK 6th and 7th editions. We've provided references to both editions because most organizations are using the 6th edition because the 7th edition is quite new.

I understand the business value this project is expected to deliver and view those benefits as significant for our organization. I actively engage with the project manager and the team to resolve issues. I accept bad news about the project without yelling, blaming, or being a disruptive colleague.

An excellent project sponsor is a vice president or an experienced senior manager whose area will benefit from successfully completing the project. The project sponsor possesses enough organizational clout to allocate resources.

High-Risk Description

I understand the worst thing that can happen to a project is an AWOL[2] sponsor. The project will flounder and not be successful without senior leadership buy-in.

The second worst thing is that multiple people are listed as project sponsors. This situation dramatically increases the team's risk of receiving contradictory statements of goals and priorities that confuse the team or lead to conflict about goals and priorities.

Another issue occurs when the sponsor is too high on the organization chart and cannot devote enough time to the position. For example, the president or CEO can't afford the time the role requires. Conversely, the team may not care what the project sponsor says when they are too low on the organization chart. For an extreme example, the intern should never act as a project sponsor for a multimillion-dollar project.

Actions to Address High-Risk Observations

Identify a project sponsor ASAP! It's probably you! If you are the current sponsor but don't think you should be, identify a better candidate. Once you have identified the project sponsor or assumed the role yourself, that person needs to meet with the team to discuss how they can support the project. Projects should never start without a project sponsor in place.

---

[2] AWOL—A military abbreviation that stands for: absent without official leave. In this case, it refers to a project sponsor that is not fulfilling their role.

Typical areas where project sponsors help include the following:

1. Ensuring various stakeholder departments commit to the resources promised in the project charter.
2. Clarifying project objectives as the details of project requirements[3] emerge.
3. Defending the team when requests to temporarily reassign specific team members to a supposed short-term emergency arise.

Please read Appendix A—Role of Project Sponsors for a more detailed discussion of the project sponsor's role.

If it's your first time acting as a project sponsor, it's okay to admit that to yourself but not your boss. Experienced project managers can coach you in the role. This book will help you develop into a better project sponsor. We're glad you're here. For more detail, please read Appendix A—Role of Project Sponsors. You may also find some of the titles in the Resources list at the end of the book helpful.

Has a Capable Project Manager Been Engaged?

The project manager is responsible for leading the project across the finish line. The project manager also connects the team to the project sponsor and steering committee.

Topic	Low-risk observations	High-risk observations
Project manager	A full-time project manager, who has my confidence, is in place. The project manager has the appropriate experience.	The project manager has other competing responsibilities. Multiple individuals share the project management role.
PMBOK references	Sixth edition: 3.4—PM Competencies, 3.3	Seventh edition: p. 4, Section 2.3

---

[3] See the Glossary entry for Requirements.

Low-Risk Description

I participated in the selection of the project manager.[4] I know who the project manager is. I am confident that the person possesses the appropriate experience and can manage the project toward success.

For example, the project manager has an established reputation for successful delivery, and the team members respect them.

High-Risk Description

Our project manager makes me nervous. High-risk project manager examples are as follows:

1. I know the project manager, but they are ineffective. They either lack the experience, technical knowledge, or leadership ability to manage the project.
2. There is no identified project manager. When I want a status update, I need to go to multiple people to understand the project's status.
3. I see that various people share the responsibility for delivering the project. There are many debates. Nothing is happening to advance the project.
4. I'm not convinced we need a project manager. They're pretty expensive, and the team seems capable of managing itself. For a description of how project managers add value, please read Appendix D—Value of Competent Project Management.

Actions to Address High-Risk Observations

Urgently engage a competent project manager if the project has no manager. Nothing useful will occur until you do. Once a candidate has been hired, meet with the person to discuss your expectations for the project. To help you describe the project manager role for a job posting or an interview checklist, please read Appendix C—Characteristics of a Successful Project Manager.

---

[4] Engaging an external project manager can be beneficial if no internal candidate offers the required experience or if an external perspective on the project goal, the proposed approach or the project technology is helpful.

If your project has an ineffective project manager, your two choices for action are as follows:

1. Appoint another project manager. This action is the fastest way to reposition your project for success but can risk morale repercussions for the team. These are much easier to address than allowing a dysfunctional project manager to continue.
2. Ask the organization that supplied the project manager to coach the existing project manager. This action will be the best way to develop a more skilled project manager, but it may delay the project's completion.

Base your choice on the status and importance of your project.

Your project manager must be highly confident that you, as a project sponsor, will support them in communicating and supporting project recommendations to stakeholders when complex issues arise. Suppose the project manager starts to sense they will be the scapegoat for project shortcomings. In that case, an experienced project manager will begin to think about how to exit the project quietly. Such an outcome can reflect poorly on the project sponsor's reputation and the team's effectiveness.

Does an Appealing Business Case Exist?

An appealing business case illustrates that the tangible benefits that a completed project can achieve are many times the estimated project cost.

Topic	Low-risk observations	High-risk observations
Project business case	There is a document that describes the project's business case. The data underlying the business case makes sense to me. I can summarize the business case as an elevator pitch.	There is no documented business case. The business case data is overly optimistic, or the business case is just a narrative. I can't summarize the business case succinctly.
PMBOK references	Sixth edition: 1.2.6, 4.1, 4.7.1, 7.3	Seventh edition: 3.4

Low-Risk Description

The business case document is complete and easily accessible. I can quickly summarize what the project will achieve. I feel good about the value we are trying to achieve.

As the project progresses, my team consults the business case to ensure project priorities and the business case are aligned. The project business case includes the following:

1. The net economic benefit of the project. Does it make sense to spend money on this project?
2. Business need. What problem does the project propose to solve? What opportunities does the project expect to capture?
3. The project goal and objectives. Are they clear and valuable?
4. Do the project goal and objectives align with the organization's strategic plan?
5. The technical and organizational feasibility of the project. Can we deliver this project?
6. A recommendation to approve or reject the proposed project.

Deciding to turn down a proposed project is *not* a failure. It's a successful outcome of the business case evaluation. Don't spend money on proposed projects when you aren't confident they will work!

Common reasons for turning down a proposed project include insufficient confidence that the project can:

1. Achieve the project goal no matter how appealing
2. Deliver enough net benefit to justify the investment in dollars and resources
3. Mitigate the identified risks sufficiently to achieve the project goal

High-Risk Description

There is no business case document. Before starting this project, no one did background research into the feasibility and purpose of the project.

If there is a business case, it's incomplete and relies upon exaggeration or even fantasy to make the project appear sufficiently valuable to attract funding.

The project sponsor and project manager can't summarize the business case in a few sentences.

Actions to Address High-Risk Observations

Starting a project without a business case is like trying to hit a bull's eye with a dart while blindfolded. You'll never reach your project goal. Your boss will likely cancel the project long before it's complete.

If your project is in the feasibility phase, now is the right time to create the business case.

If your project has started, pause and construct the business case.[5] A business analyst on the team knows how to do this. Give them the time and resources to research and build a legitimate business case.

Once the business case is complete, review it with your team. If it's not credible, improve it or cancel the project now. Only have your steering committee endorse the business case once it's credible.

Is the Project Goal Crisp and Clear?

The project goal is a compelling, business-focused goal statement that the project is expected to achieve.

Topic	Low-risk observations	High-risk observations
Project goal	I've seen a crisp, sensible, one-sentence statement of the project goal.	The project goal statement is a long paragraph. I've heard a lot of debate about goals and various conflicting statements.
PMBOK references	Sixth edition: 5.3, 5.3.3.1	Seventh edition: 2.6.2.3

---

[5] Revisiting the business case during the project is valuable because business conditions and the business environment may change. If the business case has evaporated, cancel the project.

Low-Risk Description

The project goal is valuable to the organization, in my opinion. It conforms to the SMART[6] concept. The project steering committee members endorsed the project goal.

A low-risk project goal statement is short, clear, and unequivocal. The goal statement describes business value. Low-risk goal examples are as follows:

1. Build a bridge, a factory, or a housing subdivision.
2. Develop a new product and launch it in the marketplace.
3. Implement improved inventory management to reduce perishable inventory losses to 10 percent from the current level of 20 percent.

High-Risk Description

The project goal statement does not make sense or is ambiguous to me. In my opinion, the value of the project goal to the organization is low or unclear.

A high-risk, problematic project goal statement consists of multiple sentences and aspirational or vague phrases. High-risk goal examples are as follows:

1. Build as much of the highway bridge as possible until the money runs out.
2. Encourage more employees and contractors to work from home.
3. Implement interesting or advanced technology without a compelling business goal.
4. Improve potentially awkward inventory management business processes in a yet-to-be-determined number of divisions. The solution may require custom software development. Some divisions may need to implement a new inventory management software package.
5. Clone our competitor's product but manufacture it for less.

---

[6] SMART is an acronym that stands for specific, measurable, achievable, realistic, and timely.

Actions to Address High-Risk Observations

Develop a credible project goal statement immediately. You can:

1. Ask your project manager to assemble the team and facilitate a discussion to build a clear project goal statement and agree to it. Make sure you review this statement and approve it.
2. Ensure the project manager uses the list of problems and issues that triggered the desire to embark on the project to build a clear project goal statement.
3. Take the improved project goal statement to the project steering committee to endorse it.

This discussion often clarifies the essential aspects of the project that are valuable to document in the project management plan. These clarifications typically also produce the following:

1. A list of project objectives that must also be achieved.
2. More emphasis on people change management.
3. Improved definitions for key business terminology.
4. Additions to the list of project risks that will be helpful input to the planned risk management work.

You need to intervene when a consensus on the project goal cannot be reached. Don't let your team spin its wheels in frustration. This lack of consensus occurs when the team uncovers several issues that require investigation. In this case, ask the team members to investigate and gather data or clarifications for the next meeting. Make sure you are present at this meeting. Ask the team members to present their findings without judgment. Provide your opinion on the effectiveness of the project goal. During this discussion, the team is likely to uncover more project objectives. You need to ensure those new objectives are documented as well. See the next topic for more discussion on project objectives.

So long as the goal-setting process is active, allow it to play out. Don't become impatient or frustrated and arbitrarily decree the project goal statement.

Without a firm understanding of what the project needs to accomplish, scope creep[7] will happen. You are also likely to encounter different stakeholders interpreting the project goal differently.

> Short and tangible goal statements are easier to communicate and build organizational commitment. Long-winded issue descriptions, general goodness goals, or philosophical aspirations lead to unsuccessful projects.

Do the Project Objectives Relate to the Project Goal?

The project objectives are short statements that elaborate on the project goal.

Topic	Low-risk observations	High-risk observations
Project objectives	I've seen short statements of project objectives. The project objectives support the project goal.	I've heard a lot of debates about objectives and various conflicting statements. I've heard no discussion about project objectives.
PMBOK references	Sixth edition: 1.2.3	Seventh edition: Figure 3-9, 2.6.2.2

Low-Risk Description

The project objectives make sense to me. The project objectives clarify, elaborate on, and support the project goal. The project steering committee members agree with the project objectives.

---

[7] General Colin Powell's enduring contribution to American foreign policy is the Powell Doctrine. While its purpose was to define when and how American military power should be used, it applies equally well to projects. The doctrine has three main precepts: avoid mission creep, clearly define your goal, and plan an exit strategy before you go in. See the Glossary entry for Scope creep.

A low-risk project objectives statement is short, clear, and unequivocal. Business value is described. Some low-risk objective examples are as follows:

1. Ensure people change management is implemented as improved business processes will change our employees' work.
2. Consult seriously with the citizens in the towns along the route of the new road.
3. Improve data quality to 95 percent in the new system's datastores.
4. Use only low-sulfur diesel in the trucks the project will be using.

High-Risk Description

The project objectives do not make sense or are ambiguous to me. In my opinion, the value of the project objectives to the organization is unclear or low. The relationship between the project objectives and the project goal is vague.

A high-risk set of objectives consists of vague, often aspirational, phrases that are difficult to define clearly. Some high-risk examples of objectives are as follows:

1. Utilize outsourced services where possible.
2. Ensure affected departments provide project resources as required.
3. Implement leading-edge technology where appropriate.
4. Develop the business understanding of technical employees.
5. Help employees improve their performance.

Actions to Address High-Risk Observations

High-risk project objectives are an immediate trigger to check your project goal statement. If your project goal statement is a problem, fix that first. See section "Is the Project Goal Crisp and Clear" Once your project goal statement is correct, your next steps are to:

1. Ask your project manager to assemble the team and facilitate a discussion to write clear project objectives and achieve a consensus that the list is accurate. Review these statements and approve them.

2. To endorse the goal statement and improved project objectives, take it to the steering committee.

This discussion often clarifies the essential aspects of the project that are valuable to document in the project management plan. These clarifications typically include the following:

1. A list of project in-scope and out-of-scope statements clarify the scope boundaries of the project.
2. Improved definitions for key business terminology.
3. Additions to the list of project risks that will be helpful input to the planned risk management work.

When the team cannot reach a consensus on the project objectives, the discussion will spawn several issues requiring investigation and analysis. In this case, assemble the team once the analysis deliverable is ready to be considered.

Allow this objectives development process to play out and not become impatient or frustrated and arbitrarily decree what the project objectives statements will be.

Without a firm understanding of what the project must accomplish, avoidable scope creep will happen. You are also likely to encounter different stakeholders interpreting the project objectives differently.

You have a problem if your goal statement contains more than one goal or your list of objectives is lengthy. Sometimes a goal statement is actually an objective. Move it to the list of supporting project objectives.

If you genuinely identified two goals or your list of objectives is lengthy, you may be trying to jam multiple projects into one project. That is not a recipe for success. Numerous goals and objectives suggest you may have numerous projects that are better described and managed as a program[8] of projects.

---

[8] Please read the definition for Program in the Glossary.

Is the Project Scope Well Described?

The project scope[9] description consists of multiple statements that elaborate on the project goal and objectives.

The scope statement is your team's written understanding of the work. Adding an out-of-scope description is often helpful because other distracting or appealing deliverables[10] are always adjacent to the project. This section clarifies the project boundaries and what the project won't do because there's frequent ambiguity.

Topic	Low-risk observations	High-risk observations
Scope statements	A comprehensive set of scope statements exist. The scope statements clearly state what is in-scope and out-of-scope for this project.	There is no scope statement. The scope statements are vague and incomplete. My team is unclear about what is in and out of this project's scope.
PMBOK references	Sixth edition: 5.	Seventh edition: 2.6.2.2, 4.6.5

Low-Risk Description

I've seen the scope statement, and it looks comprehensive. My team has agreed to this scope statement. The project steering committee has approved it. A low-risk set of project scope statements includes the following:

1. Detailed descriptions of what is in and out of scope
2. Titles of major deliverables

The benefit of listing what is out of scope is that it leaves much less room for interpretation of the scope statements. It helps manage stakeholder expectations and reduces the debates about scope.

---

[9] See the Glossary entry for Scope.
[10] See the Glossary entry for Deliverable.

How complicated can this be?

When we hear an initial project description, which may be no more than a quick sound bite, we often build an overly simplistic mental model of the project characteristics. That partial, inadequate, and often flawed perception lulls us into thinking the project will be easy and quick to complete. That flawed perception lulls us into making budget and schedule commitments that will embarrass us later.

Minimize the impact of a faulty initial perception by delaying commitments for as long as possible. In reality, the scope and risk of most projects are not well understood until requirements are documented, and the detailed design is mainly complete.

High-Risk Description

There is no scope statement. The team works based on their recollections of various conversations and personal understanding of the project work.

At every meeting, there is some rehashing of scope questions you thought were settled previously.

Actions to Address High-Risk Observations

You need a set of scope statements so that your team can develop a shared and unified understanding of the project work. Creating a set of scope statements is always iterative as the project team and stakeholders collaborate to refine them and work toward a consensus. Give your project team the time to establish the scope properly in the project schedule.

Some practical approaches to developing the set of scope statements include the following:

1. Listing the significant deliverable titles required to achieve every project objective. This list will make it easier for every stakeholder to appreciate and accept the changes that the project will introduce in their area.

2. Using a high-level business process[11] model to identify new capabilities and the project's changes in the organization.
3. Listing the deliverable titles required to effect the change.

You will approve the scope statement and seek the approval of the steering committee.

Misunderstanding Project Scope Is Easy

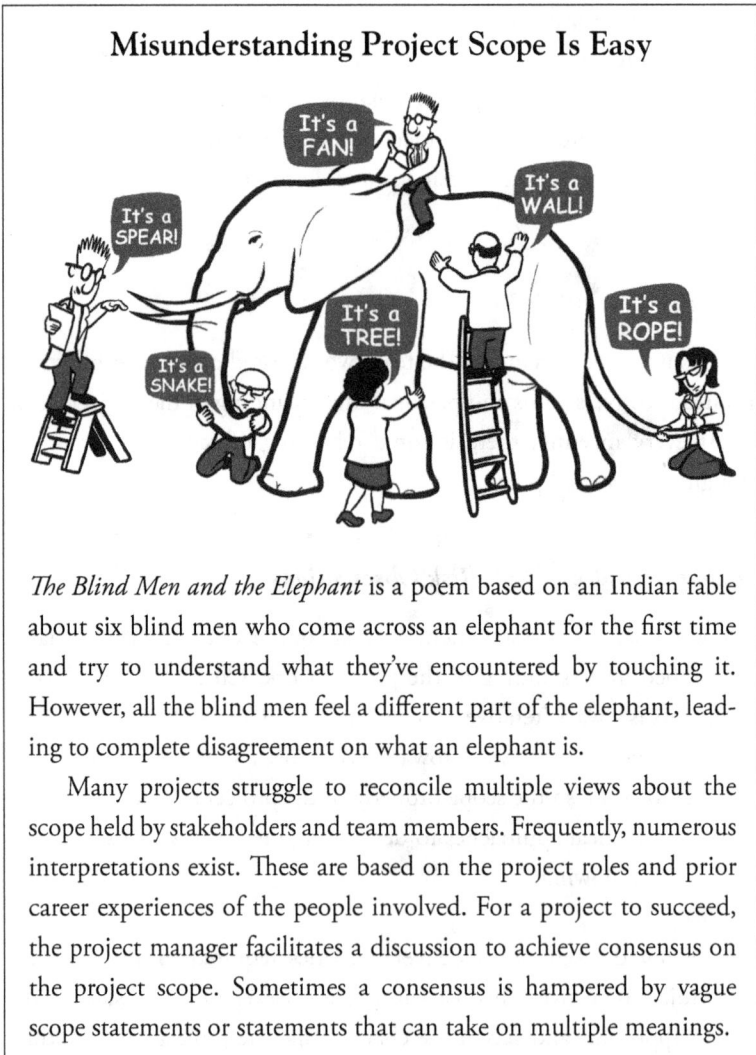

The Blind Men and the Elephant is a poem based on an Indian fable about six blind men who come across an elephant for the first time and try to understand what they've encountered by touching it. However, all the blind men feel a different part of the elephant, leading to complete disagreement on what an elephant is.

Many projects struggle to reconcile multiple views about the scope held by stakeholders and team members. Frequently, numerous interpretations exist. These are based on the project roles and prior career experiences of the people involved. For a project to succeed, the project manager facilitates a discussion to achieve consensus on the project scope. Sometimes a consensus is hampered by vague scope statements or statements that can take on multiple meanings.

---

[11] See the Glossary entry for Business process.

The project manager must stamp out the idea that everyone has a veto over decisions. While projects are not exercises in democracy, acknowledging and responding to dissent often improves outcomes. The project manager can outvote everyone on the team if necessary. A more diplomatic resolution is to create decision records.[12]

After consultation, the role of the project sponsor includes emphatic support of the project manager's decisions.

Figure 5.2 Understanding the project scope

Is the Project Charter Comprehensive?

The project charter is the formal description of the project. Among other topics, it describes the interconnections between the project organization and its business environment. Key inputs to the project charter, which motivated consideration of the project, are one or more of the following:

1. A problem or opportunity statement
2. A new regulatory requirement, often with an expected date on which implementation must be complete
3. An initiative by a competitor that requires a response

Topic	Low-risk observations	High-risk observations
Project charter	I've seen a reasonably comprehensive project charter.	The project charter I've seen is vague and incomplete. No project charter has been prepared.
PMBOK references	Sixth edition: 4.1	Seventh edition: 4.6.1

Low-Risk Description

I've read a project charter that I judged to be complete. The project manager led its development. I feel comfortable with the project description, the business value description, and deploying my organization's resources on this project.

---

[12] See the Glossary entry for Decision record.

A low-risk project charter will contain descriptive text for every heading discussed in Appendix F—Project Charter Table of Contents.

High-Risk Description

The project charter isn't raising my confidence. High-risk project charter examples are as follows:

1. There is no project charter. The team relies on their shared verbal discussion.
2. The project charter I've read is incomplete.
3. I am concerned that the business value we are trying to achieve has been significantly overstated or incompletely assessed.
4. I don't feel comfortable devoting resources to this ambiguous or overly ambitious project.

> A frequent reason for project failure is insufficient planning. To mitigate this risk of failure, invest considerable effort in developing a comprehensive project charter and vetting its contents with key stakeholders.

Actions to Address High-Risk Observations

Ensure the project manager feels supported in developing a project charter by providing the necessary inputs. They should also be given time to develop a comprehensive charter. Many reasons cause a project manager not to. Even a good project manager might not create a project charter because they:

1. Didn't receive the necessary inputs from their sponsor *cough* YOU!
2. Might not know who to ask for those inputs
3. Felt pressure to "just start the project now" and not take time to develop a project charter

To help the team develop a complete project charter, meet with your team to provide the necessary inputs to produce the charter, so come prepared. Read Appendix F—Project Charter Table of Contents to help you.

A simple Google search will also provide good project charter templates if you are unsure where to start. Your project manager should also know what's in a good project charter.

Project charter development is always a valuable exercise at any time during the project. If you are at the beginning of your project, now is the ideal time to work on a charter to clarify any potential misunderstandings about approach, scope, or business value.

Suppose your project is well underway, and this deliverable was somehow skipped. In that case, it's still a great time to work on a charter to clarify priorities, detail scope, or describe technology choices that may slow your project down.

Even if you are almost finished with your project and have avoided this deliverable, developing a charter is still a good idea. The project charter:

1. Is the basis for the project acceptance decision
2. Documents the existence and value of your project
3. Will be valuable for future reference for other projects

Creating a project charter is absolutely vital and will directly impact the success of your project. Don't be tempted to skip this step. Don't let schedule pressure cause you to think a short, superficial, or incomplete document is good enough.

Is the List of Project Benefits Appealing?

Project benefits are a list of benefits the completed project will provide to the organization.

Topic	Low-risk observations	High-risk observations
Project benefits	I can articulate the project benefits. I view the estimates of tangible benefits as reasonable.	I observe varying perceptions about the reality of project benefits. No one has had time to estimate benefits. Most of the benefits are intangible.
PMBOK references	Sixth edition: 1.2.6.2	Seventh edition: Figure 3-5, Section 3.4

Low-Risk Description

The statement of project benefits is credible to the project steering committee members and me. A low-risk statement of project benefits focuses on tangible benefits. The supporting list of intangible benefits is appealing to me.

An excellent example of a benefits statement is: We will improve customer service by reducing call center wait times by 10 percent and the cart abandonment rate by 6 percent.

High-Risk Description

Based on the documented project benefits, the project's value to the organization is unclear to me. The project steering committee members all express different ideas about the reality of the project benefits. A high-risk, problematic statement of project benefits often exhibits these characteristics:

1. Exaggerated benefits
2. Incomplete or ambiguous benefits
3. An overreliance on intangible benefits

An excellent example of a high-risk benefits statement is: We will improve customer experience. This feel-good statement lacks a quantification of the benefit and a measurement approach.

Actions to Address High-Risk Observations

To develop a comprehensive statement of project benefits, ask your project manager to lead the team to:

1. Identify, describe, and estimate the tangible benefits
2. List the intangible benefits

Understanding the benefits enables the team to make the many tradeoffs every project demands.[13] The absence of quantified benefits makes it difficult to know if a project merits approval or not.

---

[13] Read Appendix I—Triple Constraint for more detail about tradeoffs.

Once the project benefits have been identified and estimated, take a step back and evaluate if the project is even worth the resources it will consume. If you feel like it's not, cancel the project ASAP.

If you feel the project benefits are worth it, confirm that the affected stakeholders who would reap the benefits agree. Then ask your steering committee to approve the statement of project benefits.

Athens Summer Olympics—High Cost Without Lasting Benefit

It was a historic day when Athens hosted the Summer Olympics in 2004. The Greek government spent several billion dollars on facilities. Ten years later, many of the facilities were run down and abandoned. What a waste. We bet the Greek people didn't want to spend billions of dollars on abandoned Olympic facilities. We're sure they hoped those facilities would bring lasting benefits to Athenians for many decades.

If you don't scope your project properly nor define a benefits realization plan, your project will succumb to the same useless fate as the Athens Olympics facilities.

Figure 5.3 The legacy of the Athens Summer Olympics

Does the Project Budget Include All Identified Costs?

The project budget describes the estimate of the costs to conduct the project. On many projects, the highest dollar budget line item is the cost of the team effort.

Topic	Low-risk observations	High-risk observations
Project budget	I've seen the budget, and the principal line-item amounts look reasonable.	I've not reviewed or approved a project budget. The budget-line item amounts change over time. The budget I've seen shows a much lower total dollar amount than expected.
PMBOK references	Sixth edition: 3.13, 7.4	Seventh edition: 2.4.2.4

Low-Risk Description

Based on our understanding of the project approach and scope, the budget line-item amounts look reasonable to the project steering committee members and me. A low-risk project budget includes the following elements:

1. The budget is calculated using a bottom-up approach. The summary budget aggregates the cost of all the identified tasks[14] in the detailed project plan.
2. The budget shows subtotals for each phase of the project.
3. There is a contingency reserve[15] amount to cover the risk of underestimating.
4. There is a management reserve[16] amount to cover unanticipated costs.
5. There is an allowance for change orders[17] amount to anticipate the inevitable change orders. Although projects should be managed to avoid change orders, the reality is that change orders are sometimes unavoidable.
6. Most of the total cost is for the team effort. That's typical for many types of projects.

---

[14] See the Glossary entry for Task.
[15] See the Glossary entry for Contingency reserve.
[16] See the Glossary entry for Management reserve.
[17] See the Glossary entry for Allowance for change orders.

7. Other cost elements, such as allocated administrative overhead, contracted services, subcontractor work, training and travel, have been identified and included.

High-Risk Description

The budget looks incomplete. I've not seen a project budget:

1. Even though the project is well underway
2. Proposed for approval by the project steering committee and me

A high-risk project budget exhibits some of these characteristics:

1. The budget is calculated using a top-down approach based on the project phases or deliverables list.
2. The project budget amounts, or the number of budget line items, change over time.
3. There is a large contingency reserve amount to recognize the lack of detailed estimating work.
4. There is no management reserve amount.
5. There is an ample allowance amount in anticipation of significant change orders due to insufficient planning and estimating work.
6. Other costs, such as allocated administrative overhead, contracted services, subcontractor work, training, and travel, are missing or only partially estimated.

Project budgets sometimes omit or show a zero in a budget category that has not yet been estimated. This practice creates a dangerous underestimate. Any low-confidence amount, a fancy term for a guess, for all budget categories is better than a zero.

Actions to Address High-Risk Observations

Direct your project manager to lead the team to complete the project budget by developing the following:

1. A task effort estimate for every task.
2. Estimates for other cost elements such as facilities or contracted services.

Help your project by providing a rough budget range of what the organization expects this project to cost. If examples of other project budgets can be used as a guide, that's even better. This information will help your team benefit from prior experience. Every organization requires slightly different line items in their budget. If your project manager hasn't budgeted for your organization previously, they will miss something important. The more estimating resources you can give your project manager, the more accurate their budget will be, up to a point.

It's good practice to re-estimate the balance of the project at the end of every phase. Don't forget to remind the team that changes require your approval and then project steering committee approval once the initial project budget has been approved.

"Give me your best guess estimate for next year's budget. I won't hold you to it." This request leads to a politically dangerous conversation for every project manager. Providing a high estimate is seen as disrespecting the organization's finances. Providing a low estimate sets the team up for failure when they can't deliver the project for the provided amount.

We avoid providing an estimate by saying that we must complete the project charter first before giving a confident estimate. Completing a requirements analysis and a preliminary project management plan is necessary for larger projects before you can provide a confident estimate.

However, the person asking still needs a number now. Then provide an estimate for the feasibility phase of the project only.

Estimating Is Never Easy

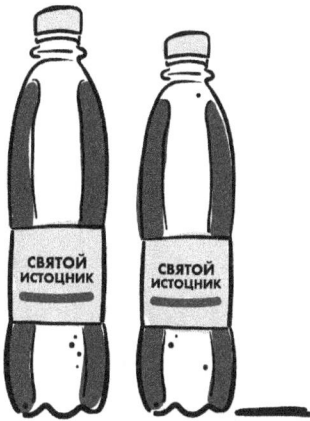

Your authors took a river cruise from St. Petersburg to Moscow, Russia, in the summer of 2016. The tap water in Russia was not potable, so we regularly purchased bottled water from the bar. Yogi bought two 1.5-liter water bottles on our first day, declaring, "This will last us for the whole day." Jocelyn was skeptical, replying, "We shall see." After we finished breakfast and filled our water bottles for our backpacks, the first 1.5-liter bottle was empty. Yogi's estimate of how quickly we would consume water was significantly off.

The moral of this story is that only someone well versed in the planned work can produce credible estimates. Teams with limited experience in the planned work will create lower-confidence estimates. These add risk to the project.

Stakeholders often judge the initial estimates as too high, pushing the team to lower their estimates. However, postproject reviews repeatedly demonstrate that the rough initial estimate was closer to reality than the lower approved estimate.

Figure 5.4 Purchasing bottled water

Summary

The purpose of the feasibility phase is to perform enough analysis to determine that the project is:

1. Worthwhile for the organization to allocate resources
2. Reasonably described and organized

The most common feasibility problem is overestimating project benefits while underestimating project costs.

CHAPTER 6

Planning

Overview

Planning is the project phase that plans how the team will develop the project deliverables.

In their eagerness to move forward, organizations tend to abbreviate planning.

A System Implementation Encounters Unexpected Difficulties

The Canadian federal government wanted to replace its badly outdated payroll systems. Successive governments pushed ahead with the Phoenix payment system rollout while ignoring the repeated pleas from the Public Service Alliance of Canada (PSAC), the union for federal public employees.

Due to technical glitches and a general lack of preparation, more than 80,000 of the 300,000 public servants have been underpaid. The project struggled to understand the details of a myriad of union agreements between the federal government and PSAC that govern pay, benefit plans, and pension contributions.

IBM, the successful vendor for the project, has not been shy about initiating many change orders to handle a multitude of

---

(Continues)

(*Continued*)

> complexities not referenced in the original requirements docu-
> ments issued by the federal government as part of the request for
> proposal (RFP) process.
>
>   As a result of inadequate planning for a complex project, it's
> now years behind schedule and billions over budget. All public,
> nonprofit, and private organizations tend to pressure themselves to
> shortchange planning to show progress on more tangible delivera-
> bles and hope for an earlier project completion date. That pressure is
> always short-sighted.

Figure 6.1 The flawed Phoenix payroll system

Is the Project Management Plan Sufficiently Detailed?

The project management plan describes how the project will run in considerable detail.

Topic	Low-risk observations	High-risk observations
Project management plan	I've reviewed the project management plan, which looks complete.	I've not seen a project management plan. The project management plan feels incomplete or vague, or ambiguous. Various documents contain different parts of the project management plan.
PMBOK references	Sixth edition: 4.2	Seventh edition: 4.6.3

Low-Risk Description

I've reviewed a complete project management plan in a single document. It answers my questions about how the project will proceed and who will do the work. I have asked the subject matter experts (SMEs)[1] not involved with the project to review the project management plan. The project steering committee reviewed and approved the document.

---

[1] See the Glossary entry for Subject matter expert.

Depending on the size of your project, this plan might only be a few pages, or it could be multiple, clearly related 100-page documents.

See Appendix G—Project Management Plan Table of Contents for an outline and brief explanations for the list of sections a project management plan should contain.

> Many executives see the time spent planning the project as bureaucratic busywork that distracts from more valuable work on deliverables. They believe the team achieves a shared understanding of the project simply by working together in the organization's environment. Don't fall into this trap. Instead, give the team the time they need to plan. Every day you spend planning will save you a week during project execution.

High-Risk Description

The project management plan is incomplete. High-risk project management plan examples are:

1. I've not seen a project management plan.
2. The project management plan is missing some sections listed in Appendix G—Project Management Plan Table of Contents.
3. The various sections of the plan are in separate documents saved in different formats in multiple places. I can't access them all easily.
4. The plan raises more questions than it answers.
5. After reading the plan, I couldn't develop an overall sense of how the project will unfold.
6. The project steering committee debated but failed to approve the document.

> Integration is never easy. Integrating the project's product into the surrounding world or the much smaller company environment is always more complicated than planned.
> Listen to the project manager of Crossrail, London's new train line, in early 2021. "The main source of difficulties was not

tunnelling, as many had predicted before work started. That finished in 2015. The toughest challenge," says Mark Wild, the project's boss, "has been integrating a tangle of signaling systems."

Address the integration problem with a more in-depth risk assessment, detailed planning, and extra contingency.

Actions to Address High-Risk Observations

The most important support a project sponsor can give the team is enough time to plan the project accurately. Too often, we observe project sponsors that push the team to hurry the planning or even stop it to start the project work. This push is a false economy. A good project management plan should be in place before significant project work begins.

Instruct your project manager to work with the team to draft a comprehensive project management plan described in Appendix G—Project Management Plan Table of Contents. Make it clear to the team that:

1. You are happy to be consulted about issues they are uncertain about.
2. You will protect the team's time to complete this vital task.
3. You will also grease the appropriate wheels if they need specialist input for planning from consultants or other SMEs.

This project management plan should be detailed enough so that a new project manager can read the plan and understand the next steps if the current project manager is hit by a bus. Remember, changes will require an approved change order once the project management plan has been accepted.

Project Charter Versus Project Management Plan

It's easy to confuse the project charter with the project management plan. In practice, many organizations do not distinguish these two deliverables well.

Whatever you call these documents in your organization doesn't really matter. What matters more is that the content exists somewhere.

A project charter formally documents your project, describes the business value the project will deliver and provides a high-level overview of project requirements. Please read Appendix F—Project Charter Table of Contents for more detail.

The project management plan discusses how the project will be organized and run in detail with subsidiary plans such as a quality management plan, a communication management plan, or a procurement management plan. Please read Appendix G—Project Management Plan Table of Contents for more detail.

Figure 6.2 A project charter is not a project management plan

Is the Project Sponsor/Project Manager Relationship Harmonious?

Successful projects depend on a great relationship and excellent communication between the project sponsor and the project manager. These two individuals connect the team to its business environment.

Topic	Low-risk observations	High-risk observations
Project sponsor/ project manager relationship	The project manager and I understand one another's work styles. I am consulted on important issues that the team is facing at suitable intervals. The project manager and I communicate in person or over video chat regularly. I am comfortable initiating informal discussions with the project manager to keep myself well informed.	The project manager and I experience constant misunderstandings. I am consulted too much or too little about issues related to the project. The project manager and I communicate infrequently. Informal discussions with the project manager are rare and feel awkward.
PMBOK references	Sixth edition: 3.3.2, 3.4.4, 3.4.5	Seventh edition: No reference

The Project Sponsor as Imperious Bully

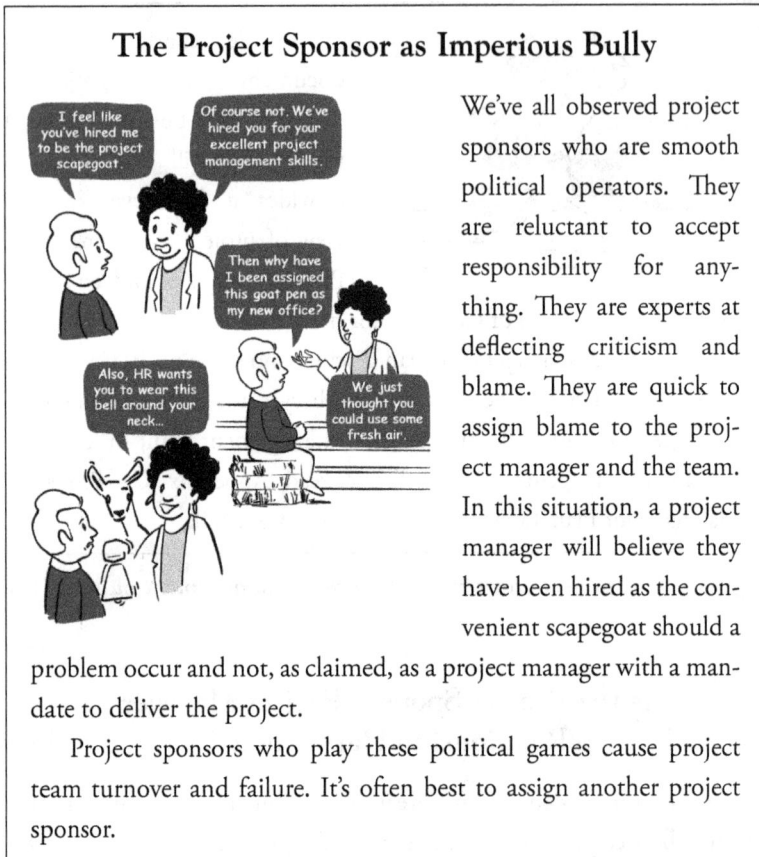

We've all observed project sponsors who are smooth political operators. They are reluctant to accept responsibility for anything. They are experts at deflecting criticism and blame. They are quick to assign blame to the project manager and the team. In this situation, a project manager will believe they have been hired as the convenient scapegoat should a problem occur and not, as claimed, as a project manager with a mandate to deliver the project.

Project sponsors who play these political games cause project team turnover and failure. It's often best to assign another project sponsor.

Figure 6.3 The project sponsor/project manager relationship

Low-Risk Description

The project manager and I understand each other's work styles and communication preferences. The project manager and I have a good relationship. A good relationship looks like this:

1. We understand each other's roles and respect those roles.
2. We communicate regularly.
3. Some of the communication occurs in a regularly scheduled in-person or video meeting.
4. The project manager consults me about important issues affecting the project.
5. The content of our communication is straightforward.

High-Risk Description

The project manager and I don't work well together. We're irritating each other. High-risk project sponsor/project manager communication examples include the following:

1. Most communication occurs by e-mail. There is little or no in-person or video communication.
2. There are constant misunderstandings due to terminology, language disconnects, or slow responses.
3. I'm consulted way too much about issues in the project. Some of the issues seem minor. I expect the project manager to deal with those without bothering me.
4. I'm not consulted enough. The team decides on significant issues that affect our organization without involving me.
5. I don't particularly like the project manager and think that person doesn't hold a high opinion of me.
6. I dread my interactions with my project manager. They always seem to take way too long for the amount of content. Sometimes it's difficult to discern what the problem is that needs attention.

Actions to Address High-Risk Observations

To improve the project sponsor/project manager relationship, create the project sponsor charter[2] that David Barrett describes. Because the project sponsor/project manager relationship is an asymmetric power relationship,[3] you need to take the initiative to meet with your project manager to discuss the behavior norms that need to be in place for you. This meeting will discuss[4] and document the following:

1. Your goals and expectations of each other.
2. Your familiarity with the role of the project sponsor. Have you held this role before?

---

[2] What is a Sponsor Charter? (https://davidbarrett.ca/sponsor-charter-3/).
[3] Read Chapter 12 for more detail.
[4] For more ideas on what to discuss, please read:
R. Bertsche. 2014. "7 Steps to Stronger Relationships Between Project Managers and Sponsors," *PM Network* 28, no. 9, pp. 50–55.

3. Your respective strengths and weaknesses.

4. Your expectation of a bias for action[5] leadership style.

5. Your preferred communication channel: in-person versus e-mail versus phone.

6. Your desired frequency of communication.

7. Format for communication. Do you prefer a narrative description of the project issues, or are briefing notes or graphs better?

Please read Appendix D—Value of Competent Project Management if it's helpful to remind your project manager how their role adds value.

If you can't achieve a smooth, professional relationship after a serious effort, you must replace the project manager.

> It's common to experience different communication styles in any team. Holding a frank discussion with your project manager upfront will save you frustration and make your job as a project sponsor easier.

Is the List of Project Resources Complete?

Project resources are the people and other resources, such as equipment, materials, and facilities, that make your project happen. For many projects, your most significant resource will be people.

Topic	Low-risk observations	High-risk observations
Project resources	The team members I've met appear to have the requisite skills and experience. The team has acquired or contracted other resources.	Multiple individuals on the team I've met appear not to have sufficient skills and experience or exhibit a good work ethic. The team has not acquired or only partially contracted for other resources.
PMBOK references	Sixth edition: p. 310, Trends and emerging practices in project resource management, 9.1.31	Seventh edition: Human resources, 2.2, 2.4.3, Physical resources, 2.5.5

---

[5] See the Glossary entry for Bias for action.

Low-Risk Description

I've observed the team members showing interest and competency in their work. In addition, a little socializing occurs between team members. Indicators of low-risk project human resource management include the following:

1. Team members demonstrate the ability to complete assigned tasks repeatedly.
2. More senior team members are supervising and coaching more junior team members.

I'm aware that the team has acquired or contracted other resources.

High-Risk Description

I'm concerned we're turning off people rather than leading and developing them. High-risk human resource management examples include the following:

1. Some team members are struggling to complete assigned tasks.
2. Some team members are spending too much time socializing with each other.
3. Some of the team appear to be marginal performers assigned to the team because their manager wanted to protect other, more effective staff.
4. I've seen these observations causing project schedule delays.
5. Some tasks are not being worked on because no one has the requisite skills.
6. Actual task effort and elapsed time are well above the project plan's estimates because the wrong people are assigned to project tasks.
7. The team vaguely knows that other resources must be acquired, but little action has been taken.
8. No one is thinking about visas for team members scheduled to arrive soon.

High-risk resource management examples include the following:

1. No one is considering the facilities the project will require for materials inventory, equipment storage, and final assembly of components.
2. The starting team's space is too small for the peak team size.
3. No one is thinking about accommodations for foreign team members.

Actions to Address High-Risk Observations

Your project manager has a good sense of what people and skills are missing from the project. Use your political capital to ensure those people are assigned to the project.

If your project manager isn't sure what skills are missing, you must collaborate to strengthen project human resources. The approach is likely to include the following:

1. Assessment of team member skills.
2. Formal training for some team members.
3. Hiring more senior individuals for the team.
4. Adding contractors and consultants to the team.
5. Transferring or laying off individuals who are not working well on the team.

Direct the project manager to acquire additional resources.

Removing individuals from a team or organization is never fun. However, procrastinating the decision only allows the problem to add risk to the project. Taking these unappealing actions is one of the reasons you're paid the big bucks.

Is the Team Organization Simple?

The team organization describes roles, responsibilities, and reporting relationships. A chart often enhances the communication of the team organization.

Topic	Low-risk observations	High-risk observations
Team organization	I've seen a reasonably clear organization chart with mostly full-time employees and only a few empty boxes.	I've seen an organization chart with too many contractors, multiple empty boxes, or too many lines.
PMBOK references	Sixth edition: 9.1.3.1	Seventh edition: 3.4.3.2

Low-Risk Description

I observe a focused team; everyone knows their role in the project. A low-risk team organization:

1. Is easily understood by a simple organization chart.
2. Consists mainly of full-time employees focused on the deliverables and not distracted by other work. Such teams make the best progress.
3. Includes a few contractors and consultants who contribute specific expertise, experience, and mentor full-time employees.

High-Risk Description

The team organization is confusing me. Indicators of high-risk organizations include the following:

1. I observe a team that is confused by too many competing priorities.
2. No one I've asked is sure about their role in the project.
3. I observe a complex organizational structure that confuses me. Too much time is invested in communication within the team and clarifying roles and responsibilities.
4. I observe many part-time employees with divided loyalties to multiple projects or previous positions. This multitasking produces slow project progress.
5. I observe too many contractors and consultants that create a knowledge gap. These individuals will eventually leave and take their knowledge with them. The knowledge gap can make it difficult for the organization to operate and sustain the product or service that the project will create.
6. I observe too many vacancies in the project organization chart. These vacancies slow project progress significantly.

Part-Time Team Members in a Matrix Organization

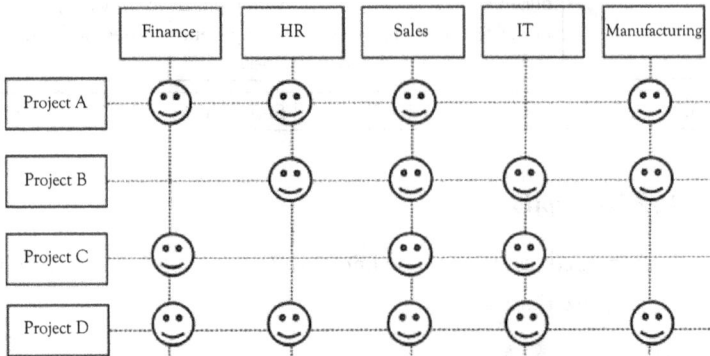

Guiding part-time employees to work effectively on multiple projects can consume too much project manager time relative to the value produced for the project.

Many organizations now operate in a matrix organization model, illustrated as follows. This matrix adds further complexity and can confuse team members about who their boss is. This issue becomes exponentially more complex when people work on multiple projects simultaneously. If this complexity exists in your organization, ensure project managers specifically and frequently tell their teams which of their various managers they report to organizationally.

To reduce speculation about what work is the highest priority, it's helpful to let your team know that the project manager will contribute to their annual review.

Figure 6.4 Project assignments in a matrix organization

Actions to Address High-Risk Observations

Simplify the team organization. Reduce the number of part-timers. Experience shows that part-timers who allocate less than 50 percent of their time to a team produce little. This lack of contribution occurs because part-timers expend the same effort on orientation, supervision, and communication as full-timers. After that, there is no time left for part-timers to perform actual work.

If too many part-time employees are dominating your project organization, ask the project manager to:

1. Reduce the number of part-timers by removing them from the team.
2. Increase the number of full-timers by negotiating for more of their time.

If too many contractors or consultants are dominating your project organization, ask the project manager to:

1. Reduce the number of contractors and consultants by replacing them with more full-time employees.
2. Hire additional employees.

These actions often require reassignments, budget reshuffling, and backfilling that will meet resistance from impacted stakeholders. To adequately resource the project and support the project manager, you must negotiate with stakeholders to overcome the likely resistance.

Use Business Analysts

Jocelyn works with a busy heart failure cardiologist, who we will call Dr. Patel. Dr. Patel runs two medical service lines at two different hospitals. If you look at her schedules for both hospitals, she is allocated 120 percent, excessive even for a physician.

Jocelyn ran a project where Dr. Patel was an SME team member. Dr. Patel wanted to be involved in the project but didn't have time to complete the day-to-day project tasks. The best way to involve her was as a reviewer and approver. So, the team hired a research analyst to complete as many of Dr. Patel's project tasks as possible. That meant preparing outlines and summarizing background medical research. Then Dr. Patel would review and put the final touches on the deliverables. Deadlines are being met more reliably since we introduced this change to project roles.

Figure 6.5 Supporting busy SMEs

Is the Project Technology Straightforward?

Project technology describes which technologies the team will employ to design, build, and implement the product.[6] Examples of commonly required technologies include the following:

1. Manufacturing
2. Distribution
3. Robots
4. Resource extraction
5. Information management
6. Information and communication technology

Topic	Low-risk observations	High-risk observations
Project technology	The team consistently uses a shortlist of technologies. I can conceptually describe the technologies.	The team uses an extensive and changing list of technologies. New technology buzzwords abound in discussions.
PMBOK references	Sixth edition: 2.2.1, 4.3.2.2, 4.4.1.5, 9.4.2.3, 11.1.3	Seventh edition: No reference

Low-Risk Description

I understand the technology that is being used by my team, at least conceptually. The team consistently references the same technology throughout your project. A low-risk description of project technologies is indicated by the following:

1. Use of a consistent technology vocabulary
2. Little planned work to select new or emerging technology

---

[6] Project technology is about the technology required to create the product. It's not about technology used to manage the project.

High-Risk Description

The team is discussing too many technologies. A high-risk description of project technologies is indicated by the following:

1. Your team constantly pushing to upgrade to more recent or different technology.
2. Requests to change from implementing off-the-shelf technologies to newer or emerging technologies.
3. The team frequently using new terminology to describe the project.
4. The team spending effort selecting new technology when the project planning work did not identify tasks for selecting technology.
5. Adoption of newly introduced technology triggering significant rework of signed-off deliverables.

On some projects, the use of new, unproven technology is unavoidable. In this case, the detailed project plan will include additional tasks and effort to:

1. Conduct more thorough testing of the technology
2. Install new vendor upgrades of the technology
3. Interact with vendor staff for technical problem resolution

Actions to Address High-Risk Observations

Clarify the technologies. Ask the project manager to:

1. Meet with the team to decide what technology needs exist for the rest of the project. Technology changes after achieving this consensus should be small and require a formal change request.[7]
2. Identify project technologies that the team wants to replace. Agree to changes only if the current technology exhibits significant shortcomings.
3. Confirm that the existing and proposed project technologies can produce the required project deliverables.

---

[7] See the Glossary entry for Change request.

Once the project technologies list is finalized, ensure you understand it, at least at a conceptual level. Reading a few articles from a Google search and watching relevant YouTube tutorials will help you feel more comfortable discussing the project technologies if anyone asks.

Don't allow the project manager or the team to intimidate you with jargon-filled answers when you express concerns about the state of the project. Instead, insist that the team describe how the technology choices support achieving the project goal and objectives.

Is the Project Schedule Realistic?

The project schedule delineates when tasks will be performed, their planned completion date and the precedence relationships among the deliverables.

Topic	Low-risk observations	High-risk observations
Project schedule	I've seen a comprehensive project schedule visualized as a Gantt chart. The schedule is available and understood by the team.	I haven't seen a comprehensive project schedule. The team doesn't appear to understand the project schedule. The Gantt chart of the project schedule changes materially from one report to the next.
PMBOK references	Sixth edition: 6.5	Seventh edition: 2.4.2.3

Low-Risk Description

I've seen a comprehensive project schedule that accounts for various potential delays. I think the described project schedule is realistic. My team members can access the project schedule and understand the dependencies for their deliverables.

For example, a reasonably clear and understandable Gantt chart visualizes the project schedule. I can see progress by comparing a Gantt chart from the last quarter or month to today's Gantt chart.

High-Risk Description

The project schedule does not look feasible to me. High-risk project schedule examples include the following:

1. I've not seen a comprehensive project schedule.
2. There are gaps in the project schedule without explanation.
3. My team members aren't aware of the project schedule.
4. I'm not confident that the described project schedule is realistic, mainly because I'm not confident in the accuracy of the task estimates that underlie the project schedule.
5. The project schedule relies on everything going perfectly for the whole execution of the project. I don't see a single day of slack.
6. Too many of the deliverables are all due on the same day. The Empire State Building construction schedule in Figure 6.6 Empire State Building construction Gantt chart illustrates this problem. Your Gantt charts should not look like that. Such a project schedule is a recipe for failure or significantly delayed completion.

Actions to Address High-Risk Observations

Developing a comprehensive project schedule is an essential skill for a project manager. If your project manager can't handle this task, you need a new project manager. Sometimes a stakeholder interferes with your project manager by declaring that the project must finish by a specific date, usually without knowing the actual project characteristics. As the project sponsor, you must use your political capital to push back against this deadline dictator. Tell your project manager that you support their commitment to best practices for project scheduling.[8]

---

[8] The best practice for project scheduling is to let the planning work, especially task effort estimates, calculate the project's schedule dates, including the completion date. It's poor practice to build a schedule by jamming tasks together to achieve an arbitrary project completion date.

Instruct your project manager to develop a comprehensive and realistic project schedule. This schedule can be produced by consulting with the team, examining other example project schedules, and asking SMEs. Your team will need time for thoughtful analysis to create a comprehensive schedule. Make sure to give it to them and don't rush it.

Do not simply add 10 percent extra days to the schedule because you know delays are inevitable. Instead, your schedule should make meaningful allowances for delays at various points by adding multiday tasks with zero effort assigned to the project manager.

The World's Highest Gantt Chart

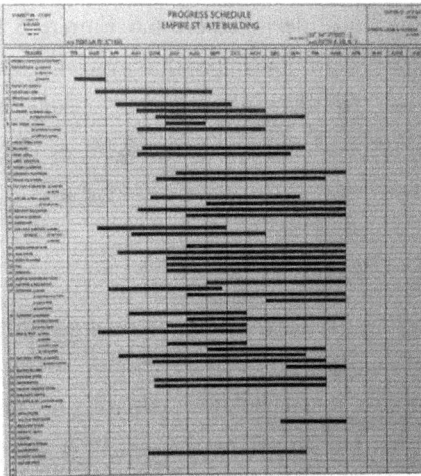

Your authors once visited the Empire State Building in New York City. While most tourists enjoyed the stunning views, we couldn't help but notice this scary Gantt chart titled *Progress Schedule* on display. As you can see, many trades were scheduled to end simultaneously at the beginning of April. While the Empire State Building was considered a spectacular and innovative construction success then and now, be skeptical if the Gantt chart for your projects looks like this.

A best-practice Gantt chart has a diagonal left-to-right appearance. This one is more vertical, with most taskbars stacked on top of each other. Scheduling work for as much parallelism as possible is an excellent technique for compressing project elapsed time. However, overdoing parallelism introduces a significant risk of schedule delay when some unexpected risk becomes a reality.

Click to read the Case Study (www.alignconsultingsolutions.com/ musings/2018/2/26/case-study-the-empire-state-building) about The Empire State Building construction written by Align Consulting Solutions on February 26, 2018. This document contains excellent project scoping and management guidance.

Figure 6.6 Gantt chart for building the Empire State Building

Are the Effort Estimates Wildly Optimistic?

Effort estimates describe how much human effort is needed to accomplish every project task.

Topic	Low-risk observations	High-risk observations
Effort estimates	I've seen effort estimates for tasks and believe them to be reasonable.	I've not seen many effort estimates for tasks. I'm concerned that available estimates tend to be duration estimates.
PMBOK references	Sixth edition: 6.2.2.2, 6.4	Seventh edition: 2.4.2.2, Figure 2-17

Low-Risk Description

I've observed that the team members assigned to the various project tasks create effort estimates. Team experience is sufficient to develop confident estimates. Creating effort estimates has produced better task definitions and new assumptions about the project details. As a result, task and deliverable completion dates are met consistently. I'm confident the team is not overworked.

Example Task Effort Estimate for a Conceptual Design Deliverable

Task names	Person assigned	Effort in hours
Confirm requirements	Jorge	4
Design	Helen	20
Engineering	Amir	15
Quality assurance	Steve	10
Human resources	Daiyu	3

Figure 6.7 Example effort estimate table

High-Risk Description

Effort estimates are missing or fluctuate too widely. High-risk effort estimate examples include the following:

1. I've observed that the team prepared estimates at the deliverable or the project phase level. Such estimates tend to be duration estimates that underestimate project effort. Effort estimates at the task level are more accurate.
2. I've observed that someone other than the person assigned to the task prepared the effort estimates.
3. There is no clear understanding of who is assigned to which tasks.
4. No effort estimate exists for many tasks.

> If creating reasonable task estimates becomes difficult and raises many questions, it may be that your project is poorly defined in the project charter. It may also be that your project is, in fact, a research and development effort[9] and should be described as such.

Actions to Address High-Risk Observations

Ensure all tasks have reasonable estimates. Ask your project manager to meet with the team to assign all tasks to team members. Then ask the assigned individuals to create task estimates. Creating reasonable task effort estimates requires considerable effort. Sometimes teams, under schedule pressure, skip over this estimating work. However, estimating work is unavoidable to produce a reliable project schedule and budget. Your stakeholders will thank you if you give your team the space and time to complete the effort estimates.

---

[9] No stakeholder should expect high-confidence effort estimates for a research and development project.

Cost Estimating Is Not Easy

This comic strip reminds us that cost estimating can quickly disintegrate into dysfunction. Management frequently pressures teams for lower estimates. There's almost always significant uncertainty in the project effort estimates. These uncertainties will ripple into the budget and schedule. Every task effort estimate and every subcontractor estimate has an associated uncertainty range. That means every project cost estimate is more accurately a range, even if it's not presented that way.

While good planning will reduce the uncertainty range, there is a point of diminishing return from successive planning cycles. Continuing to plan beyond that leads to analysis paralysis. You must be prepared to accept some uncertainty and not beat the team up over relatively minor variances.

The key to cost management on projects is decisiveness. Every project raises many issues as the understanding of project details grows from requirements analysis and design work. Pondering the resolution of these issues for too long slows the project and adds costs for no benefit.

The most significant cost category on many projects is the value of team effort. Having the team wait for issue resolution to unfold through multiple layers of management increases costs enormously. Successful teams proceed with their work on an assumptive basis.

(Continues)

(*Continued*)

> They assume that their issue resolution recommendations will be approved by management in due course and continue working on that assumption.
>
> For example, which languages will the user interface for the new online system support? The team provides its recommendations based on an analysis of the languages spoken in the countries where the system will be deployed and proceeds on that basis. If management returns with a longer list later, the project manager will write up a change order and recommend that the additional languages be deferred to the next release of the system.

Figure 6.8 Estimating project cost

Is Risk Identification Too Superficial?

Risk identification is knowing what might be coming down the pike or can occur in the project environment that could torpedo your project.

Risk management[10] is about identifying, assessing, and mitigating risks. Multiple risks are a reality for all projects. If a project fails to manage risks adequately, the risks that become a reality will prevent the successful completion of the project.

Topic	Low-risk observations	High-risk observations
Risk identification	I've observed that the team has identified potential risks in a risk register. The work looks comprehensive to me.	I've not observed the team performing risk identification. The risk register looks incomplete to me.
PMBOK references	Sixth edition: 11.2	Seventh edition: 2.8.5

---

[10] For a more detailed discussion, please read Appendix H—Severe Project Risk Situations.

Low-Risk Description

I've scanned the risk register[11] and believe it's reasonably comprehensive. A low-risk situation is characterized by the following:

1. Risks have been identified, documented, and assigned to an owner in a risk register.
2. Risks have been evaluated for likelihood and impact.
3. The high-likelihood and high-impact risks have been discussed with the project steering committee.
4. The risk register is reviewed and updated at regular intervals.
5. The risk owners are actively monitoring the risks they are assigned.

High-Risk Description

Risk identification hasn't taken place at all. A high-risk situation is characterized by the following:

1. Few or no risks have been identified.
2. The team is ignoring risks in their eagerness to move the project forward.
3. The risk register is incomplete, not maintained, or there is no risk register.
4. The team is focused on performing project tasks with little risk awareness.
5. No risk discussion has occurred at project steering committee meetings.

It's common for teams to understand about one-third of their project exceptionally well, one-third reasonably well, and one-third of the project poorly.

Focus the risk identification discussion on the murky parts of the project.

---

[11] See the Glossary entry for Risk register.

Actions to Address High-Risk Observations

Direct your project manager to lead the team to identify, describe, document, and assign risk ownership in a risk register.[12] You and the project manager must review the high-likelihood and high-impact risks with the project steering committee. All high-impact risks need a documented action plan.

Understanding project risks, with their likelihood and impact, enables the team to anticipate, preempt and mitigate many of the risks the project is likely to encounter.

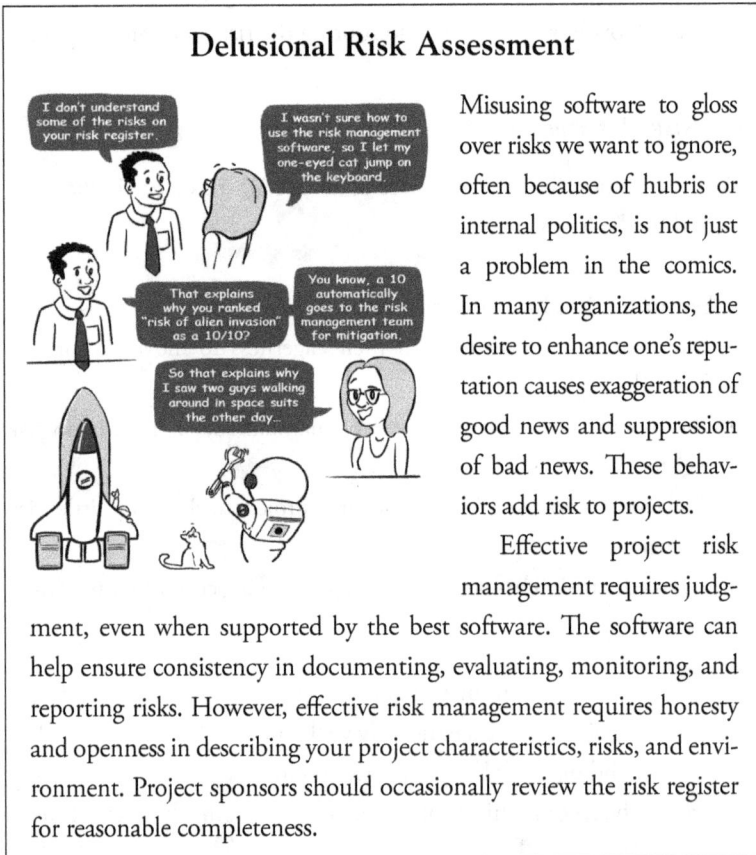

Delusional Risk Assessment

Misusing software to gloss over risks we want to ignore, often because of hubris or internal politics, is not just a problem in the comics. In many organizations, the desire to enhance one's reputation causes exaggeration of good news and suppression of bad news. These behaviors add risk to projects.

Effective project risk management requires judgment, even when supported by the best software. The software can help ensure consistency in documenting, evaluating, monitoring, and reporting risks. However, effective risk management requires honesty and openness in describing your project characteristics, risks, and environment. Project sponsors should occasionally review the risk register for reasonable completeness.

Figure 6.9 Managing project risk

---

[12] To avoid groupthink that underestimates risks, adopt this decision-making approach:
M.T. Hansen. November 22, 2013. "How John F. Kennedy Changed Decision Making for Us All." *Harvard Business Review.*

Is the Project Steering Committee Contributing Productively?

The project steering committee is responsible for guiding the project to success. This role encompasses the following:

1. Supporting the project sponsor, project manager, and team.
2. Communicating the value of the project throughout the organization.

Topic	Low-risk observations	High-risk observations
Project steering committee	The key business areas that will be affected by the project are represented. The committee meets every 4 to 6 weeks.	I don't know if a steering committee exists. Membership is unclear. Meetings are sporadic or offer little content.
PMBOK references	Sixth edition: Figure 3-1	Seventh edition: p. 180

Low-Risk Description

Our project steering committee is functioning smoothly. A low-risk steering committee is characterized by the following:

1. The presence of members representing the business functions affected by the project.
2. Meetings held at regular intervals.
3. Providing helpful feedback and assistance to the team.

High-Risk Description

Our project steering committee members are fractious or uninterested. A high-risk steering committee is characterized by the following:

1. No steering committee is in existence.
2. Frequent changes in membership.
3. No regular meetings. When the committee does assemble, the feedback to the team is not helpful.
4. The steering committee constantly suggesting new ideas or scope changes that are not helpful to the team.

Actions to Address High-Risk Observations

You need a functioning steering committee ASAP. Start by asking your team to list the business units affected by your project. Then solicit someone from those business units to participate on the steering committee. You don't want to pick someone so junior that they don't know enough about the business to be successful, but you also don't want to pick someone so high up in the business unit that they don't have time to attend the occasional meeting. Use your political clout to bring the right people into the room.

Breakfast Tacos to the Rescue

The steering committees for one of Jocelyn's projects met at 7 a.m. every other month. She ordered some lovely breakfast tacos (it's a Texas thing) and a fantastic berry bowl. The next fiscal year, a budget crunch reduced the refreshment budget. She had to scratch the berry bowl. There was a lengthy outcry from the project steering committee. Jocelyn joked with colleagues that people only came to the meeting for the berries. In the subsequent year, money was earmarked explicitly for regular berry bowls.

Small courtesies, often food, can have an outsized impact on team morale. Include a modest amount in your project budget for this.

Figure 6.10 Small courtesies bring big benefits

Is There a Consensus About the Project Goal and Objectives?

Project success ultimately depends on the support of the organization. To build support, the project sponsor, project manager, and team achieve a consensus about the project goal and objectives through communication and internal marketing.

A herculean effort by the project sponsor, project manager, and team cannot overcome opposition or lukewarm interest from the rest of the organization.

Topic	Low-risk observations	High-risk observations
Project consensus	Project team members, departments directly involved, and other stake-holders have agreed to the goal and objectives.	Whenever I speak to team members, departments directly involved, and other stakeholders, I hear substantial variations on the goal and objectives.
PMBOK references	Sixth edition: 3.3.2	Seventh edition: 2.3.3, 3.6

Low-Risk Description

The stakeholders express a consensus about the project. A low-risk consensus is characterized by the following:

1. A well-described project goal and related objectives in the project management plan.
2. The steering committee has signed off on them.
3. My team members understand them.
4. All other stakeholders know about them and have agreed that the goal and objectives provide value.

It's easier to accomplish Points 1–3. However, Point 4 is essential. Bringing all your stakeholders on board is the biggest challenge. Achieving this consensus will directly impact the successful completion of your project.

High-Risk Description

When I hear different stakeholder opinions about the project's overall purpose, I hear vastly different explanations. A high-risk situation is characterized by the following:

1. There are no documents that describe the goal and objectives.
2. If this document does exist, few stakeholders are aware of it.
3. My project team members aren't entirely sure what they are trying to accomplish.

Actions to Address High-Risk Observations

Getting to a consensus on the project goal and objectives can be challenging but essential. It's expected that everyone interprets the goal and objectives differently, wants something different from the project, and has a different view about reaching the goal. You and your project manager creatively apply your considerable soft skills to move these divergent views to a consensus.

First, ensure your project team has done an excellent job interviewing stakeholders about their needs and pain points. There should be lots of interviews with business analysts in the affected departments. If your project is public-facing or involves changes across a large organization, make sure there has been ample opportunity for the public to comment via different communication channels, including the following:

1. In-person townhalls
2. Electronic surveys
3. An e-mail address to provide comments
4. A phone number to leave a message

Second, have your team draft a document describing the project goal and objectives in detail for wide distribution. You should review this document.

Third, run that document past your project steering committee for review and approval.

Fourth, once that document is approved, you and your project manager need to turn on the charm and talk up your excitement with your stakeholders. This conversation is your chance to bring them all on board. Discuss why a specific plausible goal and related objectives were included and which were left out. Talk about why *you* are excited about the project and the value the company will achieve. Much of this promotion will occur during formal meetings about the project. Sometimes, the most effective way is in informal discussions, casual watercooler and elevator chat moments.

You are unlikely to bring every single stakeholder onto your side, especially if it's a large public works project like a new highway. You should focus your efforts on the people who will have their daily workflows changed by this project first. If you are implementing a new customer management software, you better bring your customer service reps on board or at least ensure they're not openly negative and hostile to the project.

For this reason, large organizations have a whole department involved in people change management. It can be challenging for people to change.

> Organize your project steering committee meetings with agendas and time allocations. It can be easy for steering committees to run wild with ideas or debates. But time-limited discussion topics can keep everyone on track.

Are You Planning the Acquisition of Long Lead-Time Items?

Long lead-time items are complex specialty items that few vendors make and are highly customized for every customer. Examples include bridge components, aircraft subassemblies, machine tools, and petrochemical processing equipment. These items require significant advance planning, detailed procurement work, and intense coordination with the vendor.[13]

Topic	Low-risk observations	High-risk observations
Long lead-time items	I've seen a list of long lead-time items. I'm aware of the dialogue between the team and a few potential vendors, even though a detailed design is not ready.	I've not seen a list of long lead-time items. The team knows some long lead-time items will be required but has not taken specific planning action.
PMBOK references	Sixth edition: 9.1.2.1, 11.4.2.2	Seventh edition: 2.4.6

---

[13] In most cases, project teams are aware of the long lead-time items during the planning phase. If such items surface in later phases, the project may be a research and development project that was not recognized as such.

Low-Risk Description

I've observed discussions between the team and a few potential vendors. Low-risk management of long lead-time items is characterized by early attention to the following:

1. Scheduling of specification and conceptual design tasks in the detailed project plan
2. Logistical issues associated with moving and receiving the items
3. Vendor qualification and RFP documents
4. Procurement details such as letters of intent, payment schedules, contracts, and hand-off points

High-Risk Description

I've not observed a discussion of long lead-time items. A high-risk approach to long lead-time items is characterized by one or more of the following:

1. Lack of concern about long lead-time items
2. A mistaken assumption that the long lead-time items are standard items
3. An incorrect assumption that a large quantity of stock items can be readily procured and manufactured
4. Insufficient attention to transportation logistics

Actions to Address High-Risk Observations

Ask your project manager to revise the detailed project plan to accelerate work on long lead-time items. Start engaging the vendor even though every aspect of the deliverable has not yet been defined. Often the first meeting or two with this type of vendor is more of a general description of your project. Encourage your project manager to begin the dialogue early.

Early in your project, discussions with this type of vendor will typically provide insight that will improve cost and schedule understanding.

Some on the team may push back on accelerated action by pointing out that the vendors will want more information about specifications of long lead-time items than that team has so far developed. This lack of definition is not a valid concern because early interaction with vendors is about reserving capacity in the vendor's production planning process. It's not about communicating detailed specifications.

Is There Physical Space to Conduct the Project?

All project teams require sufficient physical space to conduct the project productively. Beyond office space, many projects require shop facilities and yards to perform their work.

Topic	Low-risk observations	High-risk observations
Physical space	My team occupies a suitable physical space to conduct the project. My team has the needed desks, offices, computers, phones, and conference rooms. They have the space to store project materials when necessary.	My team is scattered throughout the building, even though working in proximity would be most efficient. Team members complain that they squeeze into a small conference room that they can only book sometimes. Insufficient warehouse space is creating logistics problems.
PMBOK references	Sixth edition: 2.2.1, 4.2.1.3	Seventh edition: 2.4.1

Low-Risk Description

My team has the physical resources to perform their work. A low-risk space is characterized by the following:

1. Everyone having a workstation
2. Space for face-to-face interactions
3. Access to the right technology resources to meet virtually
4. Access to appropriate workspaces such as laboratories or workshops
5. No one complaining about feeling squeezed into an ill-suited space

High-Risk Description

My team doesn't have sufficient suitable physical space to perform their work. A high-risk space exhibits one or more of these characteristics:

1. Some of my team members don't have desks when they really need them. I've seen team members working in the lunchroom or at picnic tables in hallways because space is at a premium.
2. A conference room booking war is in progress. No one can reliably acquire a team workspace.
3. The engineering team has been allocated a conference room when they really need space on the shop floor to do their work.
4. My virtual team members complain of constant interruptions when using the videoconferencing facility.

All these inadequacies severely limit the team's ability to be productive. Sometimes you have the right people with the right skills and experience, but they can't actually get their work done.

Many projects benefit from in-person collaboration among the team, stakeholders, and contractors. In this age of remote work and geographically dispersed teams, in-person collaboration is reduced. Compensate for this reduction with the following:

1. A superior document management system
2. Excellent audiovisual hardware and software
3. Virtual social and team-building events

Actions to Address High-Risk Observations

Space can be a problematic constraint to resolve in many organizations. More office, warehouse, or engineering space can be costly to acquire. However, paying for suitable space is less expensive than operating with a poorly performing team.

Many organizations have considerable space constraints. Here are some considerations when a space crunch must be addressed:

1. Conduct a space needs assessment for the whole team.
2. Would space changes be possible? Rearranging cubicle locations is a lot easier and cheaper than tearing down walls.
3. Is there money and time to create or renovate a better space?
4. Can you rent a nearby space for the project rather than renovating your existing space or disrupting the lives of many other employees?
5. Can you revise the onsite workday schedule for different teams? Many teams have become used to remote work with the explosion of work from home. Can you bring Team A onsite on Mondays and Wednesdays and Team B onsite on Tuesdays and Thursdays and share space that way?
6. If your virtual team members are struggling with Internet connectivity issues, it can be solved with a stipend to pay for upgraded Internet speeds at your team member's homes.

What's a Lumen?

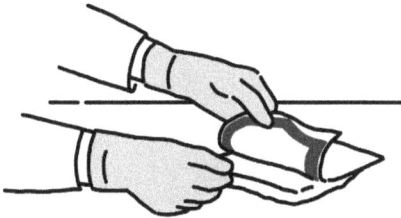

Jocelyn was a team member inspecting a new version of medical device packaging materials while working for a microbiology lab. This project visually inspected the enhanced packaging material for potential defects and validated the seam integrity.

The microbiology lab designed workrooms to let just the right amount of light (or lumens) in to perform the visual inspections. The lab assistants could then measure light levels precisely, consistently, and frequently. Accelerated aging machines were installed to predict the deterioration of the product over its typical shelf life. A whole building was repurposed for this long-term project for an important

---

(Continues)

(*Continued*)

client. New storage and warehouse spaces were renovated. This renovation made sense, given the project's length, scope, and value.

Making adequate space and facilities available for your project is a prerequisite to achieving team productivity and maintaining the schedule.

Figure 6.11 Responding to project physical space requirements

Summary

The purpose of the planning phase is to perform enough planning to ensure that the project has the following:

1. Developed a comprehensive plan
2. A complete organization in place
3. Access to required resources

The most common planning problem is underestimating task effort due to overoptimism.

CHAPTER 7

Design

Overview

Design is the project phase consisting of analysis to produce detailed designs of the project's deliverables.

Too often, projects produce incomplete designs because the requirements elicitation was not broad or detailed enough.

Misinterpretations Are Easy

Consider how easy it is to misinterpret this license plate:

One person will give the more likely interpretation as Mrs. Limo. Another person might provide a less plausible interpretation as Mr. Slimo. Do you feel like your project manager frequently acted on the Mr. Slimo interpretation when you thought you were communicating Mrs. Limo? These interpretation, assumption,

---

(Continues)

(*Continued*)

> or communication disconnects are a perennial issue across many projects.
>
> Teams wrestle with misunderstandings and misinterpretations constantly. These disconnects become more frequent when multiple languages, disabilities, cultures, and distances are involved. Those misses lead to misses about the interconnectedness of project deliverables.
>
> For example, workers speak many culturally nuanced English dialects that quickly lead to misunderstandings in our globally connected multicultural world. The challenges increase even further when team members don't have the country's primary language as a mother tongue. Good project managers must keep these nuances in mind when communicating with teams.
>
> Project managers patiently facilitate discussions to improve understanding and reach a consensus about project requirements, priorities, and direction to achieve a successful project. The role of the project sponsor is to support and encourage the project manager.

Figure 7.1 Reducing never-ending misinterpretations

Are the Project Requirements Sufficiently Detailed?

Project requirements consist of a set of deliverable requirements. Together the deliverable requirements describe what the project's product will be capable of upon project completion.

Topic	Low-risk observations	High-risk observations
Project requirements	I've seen a detailed report of functional and nonfunctional requirements.	The report of project requirements I've seen is too high-level or uneven in detail. The team has not achieved a consensus on the requirements. The report of project requirements is incredibly detailed and sounds more like a design document.
PMBOK references	Sixth edition: 5.2	Seventh edition: 2.3.3

Low-Risk Description

The team has created a detailed report of functional and nonfunctional product requirements that looks comprehensive. Business analysts, in whom I have confidence, were intimately involved in preparing the report. Based on their opinion and my review, the requirements report is credible to me. The requirements report is reasonable to the project steering committee members. A low-risk requirements report:

1. Covers all aspects of the project scope evenly
2. Describes each functional requirement in considerable detail with associated conceptual diagrams
3. Emphasizes describing the requirements and avoids detail about how the requirements will be met
4. Describes each nonfunctional product requirement with multiple sentences
5. Gives equal attention to functional and nonfunctional requirements

Functional requirements describe what the product must do. For example, if the product is a warehouse, it must accommodate the following:

1. So many tons or cubic meters of products
2. So many employees inside and in the parking lot
3. So many rail cars and trucks and related loading and unloading capacity
4. Use of robots with specific characteristics
5. Storage of products under specific temperature and humidity conditions

Nonfunctional requirements describe how the warehouse will be implemented or must perform. Good examples include the following:

1. Load and unload so many rail cars and trucks concurrently.
2. Accommodate a maximum rate of product movement within the warehouse.

3. Compliance with applicable safety codes, building codes, and fire codes.
4. Accommodate employees with some disabilities.
5. Handle interior and exterior temperature, wind, and other weather fluctuations.
6. Concrete can only be poured under specific temperature ranges and other weather conditions.
7. Construction and commissioning can or cannot occur at night.

The Glossary contains definitions for Requirements—functional and Requirements—nonfunctional.

Often, project sponsors cannot be close enough to project details to know if the requirements are comprehensive. Ask experienced business staff not part of the team to review the detailed requirements and offer an independent assessment.

High-Risk Description

The project's requirements are incomplete, unclear, and not acceptable to me. A high-risk requirements report often exhibits one or more of these characteristics:

1. Covers the project scope unevenly.
2. Describes requirements in a cursory manner.
3. Focuses on either functional or nonfunctional requirements to the exclusion of the other.
4. Contains many generic statements that likely were copied directly from another similar project without further analysis.
5. Assembled from multiple web pages, monographs, and vendor papers without adaptation to the project characteristics.
6. Is hugely detailed and lengthy. It goes beyond what is required and describes how the requirements will be met. That makes it sound more like a design document.

Sometimes, teams are rebuffed when seeking to elicit requirements. They are told the information is only provided on a *need-to-know* basis, and the team's request doesn't qualify.

This lack of open communication is a high-risk situation that will increase project effort and undermine success.

The project sponsor must push back. If the information is still not forthcoming, the project sponsor can reduce the scope accordingly. Trying to limp along without the information is more likely to waste money than produce valuable results. In extreme cases, it may be necessary to cancel the project.

Actions to Address High-Risk Observations

Ask your project manager to lead the team to elaborate on the requirements and fill in the gaps. Achieving a consensus on requirements is often tricky. The discussion will spawn many topics that require investigation and analysis. The analysis will become the basis for the following:

1. Clarifications and conclusions about how the product will operate that the team will document in the requirements report
2. Project scope clarifications
3. Resolution of business issues and related recommendations that require the approval of the project sponsor and other stakeholders

As the project sponsor, you need to help the team if questions cannot be settled with stakeholders. Ensure the team has the resources they need to define the requirements adequately.

Orange Juice Recipe Requirements

Too many projects fail due to inadequate, cursory, or incomplete project requirements. Very few fail due to complex or overly detailed project requirements.

(Continues)

(*Continued*)

To better understand excessively detailed requirements, read the Orange juice recipe (www.jocelynlapointe.com/yogis-famous-orange-juice-recipe).

Many teams feel schedule pressure and may choose to cut corners on project requirements. Project sponsors add value by defending the team's determination to produce comprehensive requirements. Project managers add value by coaching the team to stick to requirements and not delve into the design.

Figure 7.2 Comprehensive project requirements

Is Your Primary Client Enthusiastic About the Project?

For project success, the client or primary stakeholder who supported the approval of the project must continue to express that support by:

1. Communicating their enthusiasm about the benefits of the project
2. Providing the resources that your project needs

Topic	Low-risk observations	High-risk observations
Client engagement	The client consistently provides the necessary resources, such as business staff and systems, to make the project successful.	I'm aware that the team can't access the resources required to make the project successful, such as business staff, login credentials, and company policies.
PMBOK references	Sixth edition: 13	Seventh edition: 2.1.1, 3.3

Low-Risk Description

I'm confident our client is appropriately engaged. Seconded team members from the client's department play an active role. The team can access internal systems and policies. Our project is progressing well because the client provides information, issue resolution, and access to people and systems.

High-Risk Description

The client's expectations are not aligned with what the project is intended to deliver. High-risk client engagement examples include the following:

1. The client declined to assign staff to the team because the individuals are critical to the department's operation.
2. I observe the team cringe every time they need to e-mail the client for a piece of information.
3. I know it will take weeks to receive a response to a clarification question or a deliverable signoff.
4. When onboarding new team members, gaining access to the client's databases or e-mail system takes weeks. Sometimes they can't even acquire an ID card to let them pass security. Yikes!

> One of your authors recalls a project where it took 4–5 months for a team member to receive all the building and system accesses required to perform the job the client was paying for.

Actions to Address High-Risk Observations

There is no simple one-size-fits-all solution to maintaining engagement. You and the project manager should meet with the client, preferably the person who signed the deal and explain the situation. Depending on the size of the client, you may need to persuade several departments onto the same page and fulfill their commitments.

Here are a few things you can do on your end:

1. Backfill the individuals needed on the team with contractors in the client department.
2. Document delays in fulfilling information requests. Going to the client with the facts about what delays have occurred and what requests were made is a CYA move, but it can also inspire action on the client's part. Maybe they've never seen it all spelled out before.
3. Create a customized consultant role in your client's system. This role will ensure incoming team members have the same access as all other team members. You won't need to go system by system to provide access individually.
4. Make a new flow chart and checklist for onboarding team members.
5. As a last resort, offer to delay the start of the project until the client is ready to support it. This delay may lead to project cancelation. However, that may be preferable to project failure caused by inadequate support.

Food Solves All Problems

Consider employing the simple cupcake or the humble latte to your advantage. Bringing a small token of appreciation to a crucial individual can make a world of difference. We don't like to admit the need for a little *grease* to advance the work. But putting yourself on the good side of someone in the access management department can only help. Jocelyn has baked many batches of influential cupcakes in her career.

Project sponsors can emulate this example by regularly buying pastries or lunches for the team.

Figure 7.3 The role of food in projects

Are Internal Politics Threatening Your Project?

Internal politics[1] are unavoidable. Competition for status or power drives internal politics. Competition is a two-edged sword that produces progress and innovation while simultaneously creating incentives to burnish one's reputation and assign blame. Too often, those who are more confident and outspoken attract more support and achieve more success with that support. Many good projects have failed because the politics weren't managed appropriately. Addressing these concerns can be frustrating and distracting, but your goal of a successful project requires it.

Topic	Low-risk observations	High-risk observations
Internal politics	I've heard stakeholders make supportive comments about the project. When I enlisted the help of stakeholders, they completed the agreed actions.	I've heard stakeholders make critical comments about the project. I've heard derisive comments about the project manager and individual team members. When I enlisted the help of stakeholders, they listened politely but didn't agree to take action.
PMBOK references	Sixth edition: 2.4., 3.3.3	Seventh edition: 4.2.4.3

Low-Risk Description

The project manager and I are proactively meeting with stakeholders to communicate project status, correct rumors, and gauge attitudes toward the project. We are hearing constructive comments about the project and responding to those expeditiously.

High-Risk Description

Our stakeholders are avoiding the project manager and me. High-risk internal politics indicators include the following:

1. Some team members have transferred away from the project.
2. Some project steering committee members are sending a junior representative, claiming they don't have time to attend.

---

[1] See the Glossary entry for Internal politics.

3. Finance and audit are taking an unusual amount of interest in the project.
4. E-mails are not being answered or are answered late with noncommittal responses.
5. Individuals we are trying to recruit for the team are declining our requests.
6. Some individuals hoard information that would help the project.

Actions to Address High-Risk Observations

You and the project manager can counter negative internal politics with your own action plan. You can't delegate this work to project team members. Consider which of these actions are relevant to your situation:

1. Ramp up your project communication and internal networking.
2. Align yourself with the senior managers that approved the project and have continued to support it.
3. Prioritize responding to senior managers who are likely members of your steering committee.
4. Provide senior managers with timely, appropriate, and constructive project information that's diplomatically phrased.
5. Keep the project goal and objectives in mind. Unceasingly articulate why those are best for the organization.
6. Listen carefully to how your message is received. The more information and knowledge you can gain about subtle organizational themes, the better you'll align your messaging and priorities with those of other departments.
7. Don't gossip or spread rumors.

Before Jocelyn saw the light and became a project manager, she spent time in the performing arts. During a performance, one of Jocelyn's colleagues didn't realize his mic was still on after he went backstage and began complaining about a scene that didn't go well. He used several curse words that were broadcasted to the whole audience. Someone backstage quickly put their hand over his mic, but the damage had occurred. He had a hot mic incident. When communicating with colleagues about any project, operating like you constantly wear a hot mic is best. Would you like to broadcast what you are saying about the project, yours or a colleague's, to the PA system at work? If not, perhaps it's best to keep it to yourself.

Pizza! Hold a project kickoff meeting, invite all stakeholders, and serve pizza and soft drinks. This small act will bring many people into the room. Some will be meeting in person for the first time. Now you can tell them all about your project. The introductions and the information will have lasting benefits.

Has Your Project Engaged With Affected Stakeholders?

Stakeholder engagement is the art of keeping your stakeholders happy.

Topic	Low-risk observations	High-risk observations
Stakeholder engagement	I know that affected stakeholders know our project is actively underway. I've seen a list of the affected stakeholder groups with the current contact.	I'm aware that affected stakeholders don't know who the project manager is or that a project affecting their work is underway. The list of the affected stakeholder groups is incomplete.
PMBOK references	Sixth edition: 13	Seventh edition: 3.3, 2.1.1, 2.1.1.4

Low-Risk Description

I've seen the stakeholder engagement plan, and I see my team implementing it. I can tell the stakeholders are engaged because:

1. There is representation on the project steering committee and the team.
2. Stakeholders know I'm the project sponsor of a project that affects them. They also know the name of the project manager. When

the project manager or I e-mail them, I don't receive a reply like "Who are you, and what do you want?"

3. They are happy the project is happening.

High-Risk Description

Our stakeholders are too immersed in their own work to fulfill their role in the project. High-risk stakeholder engagement plan examples include the following:

1. I've not seen the stakeholder engagement plan.
2. The stakeholder register looks incomplete, with out-of-date contacts.
3. The stakeholder engagement plan I've seen is incomplete or vague.
4. The team isn't implementing the stakeholder engagement plan.

Stakeholders that the project will affect are ignoring me. High-risk stakeholder indifference examples include the following:

1. My project languishes in obscurity.
2. The stakeholders it affects are unaware of the project.
3. The leaders of some stakeholders don't know who I am or who the project manager is. As a result, any e-mail to these stakeholders for project input is met with surprise.
4. Affected stakeholders make many excuses for not fulfilling their previously agreed commitments to the project.
5. Affected stakeholders know about my project but are against it and hostile to the team and me.

> A Google search for stakeholder engagement plans is a great place to find examples when writing a stakeholder engagement plan from scratch.

Actions to Address High-Risk Observations

Ask your team to develop a stakeholder engagement plan. You may need to start by identifying the stakeholders you know to jumpstart the team's thinking. Don't rush this portion of the project.

Instruct your project manager to perform a stakeholder identification and analysis exercise. You and the project manager should meet with the identified stakeholders to explain the project and seek their input. More complex projects involve multiple senior executives. Make sure you identify them all.

As your project unfolds, you will likely uncover additional stakeholders that were missed initially. Don't panic. Do your best to update your stakeholder engagement plan and bring those stakeholders up to speed.

For hostile stakeholders, be patient and sensitive to bring them on board. Meet to discuss their issues with the project. Often people are worried about their budget and their jobs when changes loom. Make assurances where you can, but don't lie. You may need to discuss the concerns with the project steering committee.

Are You an Effective Communicator?

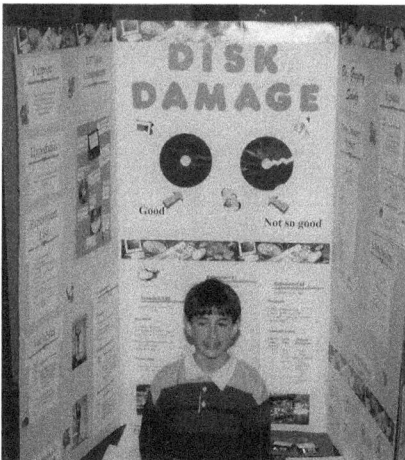

One Saturday morning, the Schulz family arrived at a large auditorium to set up their projects at the annual science fair. The Schulz children were enrolled in the French Immersion Program. So, they carried poster boards with their science projects described in French. Gregory, on the left, is seated with his project display.

Yogi had signed up to be an English Language science fair judge, knowing he would not be asked to judge his children's French projects. But when Yogi arrived, one of the French Language judges was AWOL. So, he volunteered to judge the French science projects. It was a complete disaster. Yogi had vastly overestimated his ability to communicate in French, especially with all the scientific terms. He

(Continues)

(*Continued*)

was grateful that two other native French-speaking judges were on the panel and deferred to them.

Just like Yogi overestimated his French communication skills, it's easy for everyone to overestimate their skills in communication. Whatever amount of project communication you are planning or doing, it's never enough. Do more!

Figure 7.4 Overcommunication is impossible

Is Someone Monitoring the Known Project Risks?

Risk monitoring[2] is about reviewing the status of identified risks and the comprehensiveness of the mitigation tasks planned to address high-likelihood and high-impact risks.

Topic	Low-risk observations	High-risk observations
Risk monitoring	I know that the team reviews project risks and regularly updates related mitigations.	I am aware that the team reviews project risks rarely or never.
PMBOK references	Sixth edition: 11.7	Seventh edition: 2.8.5. Figure 3-11

Low-Risk Description

I've scanned the risk register and believe it's reasonably current. A low-risk situation is characterized by the following:

1. A risk register that is reviewed and updated with monitoring results at reasonable intervals.
2. Mitigation tasks for new high-likelihood and high-impact risks are updated in the detailed project plan and performed.
3. A single team member being assigned to each risk and monitoring it.

---

[2] For a more detailed discussion, please read Appendix H—Severe Project Risk Situations.

Don't forget to update the lessons learned register[3] once you've completed a risk mitigation task. Future colleagues will appreciate your insight into the effectiveness of that mitigation work.

High-Risk Description

I'm not observing any work that might be risk monitoring. High-risk risk monitoring examples include the following:

1. I've not seen the risk register. I wonder if one exists.
2. The risk register I've seen is not up to date with monitoring results.
3. The risk register has not been reviewed and updated since it was initially created.
4. A group of people or no one owns various risks. This unclear ownership means no one is taking responsibility for monitoring that risk.

Actions to Address High-Risk Observations

Ask your project manager to lead the team to review the risk register at reasonable intervals. Ensure that one person owns every risk and those owners review their risks at specific intervals.

A significant number of risks are a fact of life for most projects. Ensure those team members responsible for risk ownership have assigned tasks to review risks. If they are overallocated with other work, the risk-related tasks will be pushed to the back burner.

Risk monitoring is a task that many teams abandon when the pressure to meet a milestone[4] date increases in intensity. A good response is to schedule risk monitoring early in every phase rather than later.

---

[3] See the Glossary entry for Lessons learned register.
[4] See the Glossary entry for Milestone.

Is Your Product and Service Procurement Consuming Too Much Effort?

Product and service procurement involves identifying and assessing vendors' suitability and capability to work on project deliverables.

You need vendor selection criteria that are more robust than "Guy with the best moustache."

Topic	Low-risk observations	High-risk observations
Product and service procurement	I'm aware of a reasonably rigorous process for procuring products and services.	I'm aware of an arduous and excessively rigorous process for procuring products and services. I've observed that the team procures products and services based on personal relationships.
PMBOK references	Sixth edition: 12	Seventh edition: 2.5.6

Low-Risk Description

I've observed that the team spends little effort on product and service procurement. The following observations characterize our product and service procurement as low risk:

1. Our selection methodology is proportional to the quantity and complexity of the items we buy. Methods for acquiring office supplies are less rigorous than those used for procuring enterprise software packages or major construction services.
2. Our vendors are not complaining about our procurement process.
3. The procurement group is respecting my award recommendations.
4. We are paying our vendors on time.

High-Risk Description

Procurement tasks distract valuable team members from working on other deliverables that I view as more important. High-risk product and service procurement examples include the following:

1. I've observed the team spending a lot of effort on product and service procurement.
2. We are procuring products and services with poor definitions.

3. The selection criteria for evaluating vendors, products, and services are incomplete or too general, leading to protracted debates and indecision within the team.

4. I've observed lots of procurement process complexity that consumes significant team effort.

5. I've observed the procurement group thinking they're in charge of awarding business to vendors, despite accepting no accountability for results.

6. I've heard that vendors express their disdain for our process, perhaps in a veiled way.

Actions to Address High-Risk Observations

To reduce procurement efforts, work with your team to improve the following:

1. Definition of the products and services to be procured. If these definitions are vague and murky, it often indicates the requirements document is inadequate.

2. Selection criteria for evaluating vendors, products, and services.

Ask yourself if you can simplify the procurement methodology without materially increasing risk. If your organization has a procurement group, talk to them about their arduous process and explore opportunities to streamline it. Your current and future project managers will sing your praises if you can simplify the organization's procurement process.

All I Need Is a Credit Card

Cartoons often exaggerate real life. Too many believe the procurement group acts as a blocker preventing all purchasing.

Procurement management is valuable when it reduces risk, avoids corruption, and ensures organizations receive value for their expenditures.

(Continues)

(*Continued*)

Figure 7.5 Managing procurement risk

Is Vendor Contracting Generating a Lot of Debates?

Vendor contracting involves negotiating and executing contracts for project-related products and services with successful vendors. Contracting occurs after the selection and award processes are complete.

If you are contracting with major companies, you will end up signing some contracts you don't like because these vendors assign all the risks to you. Agonizing over that won't help advance the project.

Topic	Low-risk observations	High-risk observations
Vendor contracting	I'm aware of a reasonably structured process for contracting with vendors.	I'm aware of a horrendously complex process for contracting with vendors that consumes significant team effort.
PMBOK references	Sixth edition: 2.2.1, 12	Seventh edition: 2.4.6

Low-Risk Description

I've observed that the team spends little effort on vendor contract development. Low-risk vendor contracting examples include the following:

1. The vendor contract's complexity is proportional to the complexity of the products and services being procured.
2. Acceptance of the vendor contract, even though it places all the risk on the customer when there is no reasonable prospect of revising the contract terms.[5]

High-Risk Description

I've observed the team spending a lot of effort on vendor contract development. High-risk vendor contracting is characterized by the following:

1. Poor definition of the products and services in the contract.
2. Lots of negotiation and contract drafting complexity that consumes significant team effort.
3. Lawyers and procurement staff raising many concerns and low-probability risks that are almost impossible to resolve to their satisfaction. These concerns create distraction and delay for the team.
4. Vendor marketing staff taking the project sponsor and project manager golfing to dissuade them from requesting contract revisions.

---

[5] When you're contracting with major vendors, these companies are not the least bit interested in your proposed changes to their standard contract. You are forced to accept the contract and whatever risks it assigns to you. If the risks you see in signing the vendor's standard contract are unacceptable to you, you must find another vendor. Don't invest precious time in attempting to revise the vendor's standard contract.

Actions to Address High-Risk Observations

The project sponsor must educate the organization about the reality that prominent vendors expect customers to sign their contracts without much debate or discussion and certainly not negotiation.

When your organization is large and has its own lawyers to review contracts, the review delays can materially impact the project schedule. The project sponsor can be most effective by intervening on behalf of the team by asking the lawyers or their bosses to back off. Project managers usually don't have the political clout to intervene. The vendor won't accept the proposed changes even though you agree that the proposed changes will protect your organization better.

Sometimes signing a letter of intent with a vendor can take signing a formal contract off the critical path for the project. The letter of intent allows the project to proceed without waiting for lawyers and procurement staff to finalize contract details. If a project is late, no one cares that contracting delays led to the project delay. Justified or not, that outcome can make the project sponsor and team look unsuccessful, even though the project is successful.

Is Vendor Performance Disappointing?

Is your vendor delivering value on commitments? This topic is about assessing the quality of vendor performance.

Topic	Low-risk observations	High-risk observations
Vendor performance	I've seen information about the vendors' timeliness and quality of deliverables that I assess as acceptable.	I've seen information about the unacceptable quality of the vendor deliverables. I've not seen information about the quality of the vendor deliverables.
PMBOK references	Sixth edition: No reference	Seventh edition: 2.5.6.1

Low-Risk Description

I've observed no indication of vendor performance problems. Low-risk vendor performance is characterized by the following:

1. On-time and on-quality delivery.
2. Vendor commitment to customer service.
3. Responsiveness to the inevitable issues that arise.
4. Reasonable discussions about plans and problems between team members and vendor representatives.
5. Rational discussions about change order scope, schedule, and price.

High-Risk Description

I've observed lots of frustrations related to vendor performance problems. High-risk vendor performance is characterized by the following:

1. Repeated deficiencies in delivery
2. Continuing negotiations of contract terms or scope well after the contract is signed
3. Tense dialogue between team members and vendor representatives about delivery defects
4. High or even ridiculous costs for change orders
5. Threats of problem escalation or legal action

Actions to Address High-Risk Observations

Ask your project manager to formally communicate the team's unhappiness with the vendor's quality deficiencies or late delivery. Contacting a senior executive at the vendor's organization can be effective when you believe your concerns are not being addressed and communicated within the vendor organization.

Depending on the depth of available vendors and your contract, you might explore switching vendors. Switching from one vendor to another can be easy if you are sourcing fungible office supplies but can be much more complicated if you are sourcing a unique component, product, or service.

Switching vendors will add cost and delay your project. So, tread very carefully. But if a vendor is consistently problematic, the disruption of switching could be worth the effort.

Ensure your organization is tracking vendor performance. When vendors need to be contracted in the future, your previous performance assessment will be readily available.

> A round of golf with a senior executive at the vendor's organization, its account representative, you, and your project manager can be more effective than another sternly worded e-mail.

Are Your Project Meetings Boring?

Meeting management is the art of holding productive meetings.

Topic	Low-risk observations	High-risk observations
Meeting management	I've seen project meeting agendas. I can find the meeting minutes.	I haven't seen meeting agendas. I can't find minutes from previous meetings, or the minutes are incomplete.
PMBOK references	Sixth edition: 10.2.2.6	Seventh edition: 4.4.3

Low-Risk Description

Meetings are scheduled well in advance on a regular, recurring basis. I've observed that meetings are run with agendas. I can easily find meeting minutes from previous meetings. Meetings end with a clear set of action items assigned to specific individuals. The status of prior assignments is reviewed at subsequent meetings.

High-Risk Description

Too many meetings are not productive. High-risk meeting management examples include:

1. No agendas are created.
2. I can't find the meeting minutes.

3. I'm not sure what the team members are discussing in their meetings.
4. I've attended a few poorly run project meetings. In the end, I asked myself, "What did we accomplish? Did we make any decisions? Who is fixing this problem?"

Don't hesitate to cancel a meeting when nothing is on the agenda. Everyone likes it when a meeting is canceled occasionally.

If cancelations occur more than occasionally, you have a communication problem that needs attention. Meetings are essential to maintain a shared understanding of the project goal, objectives, status, and issues. Improve the content of your meetings.

Actions to Address High-Risk Observations

Improve meeting effectiveness with these ideas:

1. Plan every meeting with a published agenda.
2. Implement a standard meeting agenda template across all your projects. Communicate your expectation to your project manager that the team will use the template for all meetings.
3. Document conclusions as decision records.
4. Ensure every meeting ends with a brief recap of action items. After the meeting, the project manager e-mails the action items to the team.

Certified Project Managers Can Be Dangerous

Essential skills for completing projects successfully include project management, leadership, and experience with project management methodologies. Unfortunately, as in the comic scenario, these skills can become project failure topics when misused or overused.

Project reviews and quality assurance of project deliverables are essential to successful projects that produce business value. However,

(Continues)

(*Continued*)

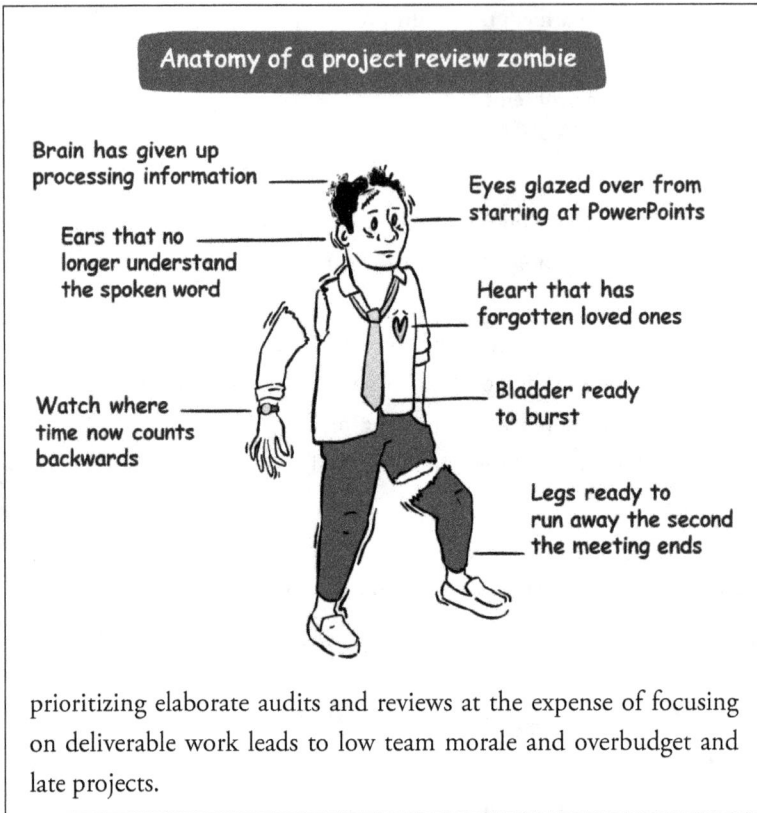

prioritizing elaborate audits and reviews at the expense of focusing on deliverable work leads to low team morale and overbudget and late projects.

Figure 7.6 Project reviews are important

Summary

The purpose of the design phase is to design the deliverables comprehensively based on the functional and nonfunctional requirements. Designs need to be explicitly and clearly described so that almost anyone off the street can understand them. Clarity is a demanding standard.

The most common design problem is one of the following:

1. Conceptual or high-level designs don't contain enough information for the detailed design and the upcoming build phase to succeed.
2. Incredibly detailed designs that cost too much and take too long to produce.

CHAPTER 8

Build

Overview

Build is the project phase that constructs the deliverables with integrated quality control tasks.

When progress is surprisingly slow, it's often because the project team is performing design work that was missed in the previous phase.

Assigning Optimal Resources for the Task

Your authors had traveled on a family vacation to visit Yogi's in-laws in San Antonio, Texas. While there, Yogi noticed the broken automatic garage door opener at his in-laws' home. Determined to be a value-add son-in-law, Yogi and his brother-in-law Jeff, a petroleum

engineer, set about replacing the garage door opener. This task took them a full day and multiple trips to the local hardware store. But by supper time, they were successful, and the in-laws were pleased with the functioning automatic garage door opener.

That evening, your authors visited Yogi's sister-in-law Marci only to discover that her garage door opener had also stopped working earlier in the week. She had called a repairman, and for $50 and 45 minutes of work, a new, functioning automatic garage door opener was in place.

(Continues)

(*Continued*)

> This story presents an essential lesson on resource management. Some of your team members might be capable of completing a task, but they aren't the optimal person. Teams are more productive when the right people are assigned to the right tasks.

Figure 8.1 Assigning project resources

Is the Product Design Sufficiently Detailed?

Product design consists of detailed descriptions, diagrams, and models that describe how the written project requirements will be turned into reality.

Topic	Low-risk observations	High-risk observations
Product design	I've seen complete detailed designs for the project deliverables.	The designs I've seen are too high-level or uneven in detail. The team has not achieved a consensus on the design of some deliverables.
PMBOK references	Sixth edition: 1.2.4.2, 2.4.4.2, 5.2.2.8, Figure 5-13,	Seventh edition: 2.3.5

Low-Risk Description

The team has created detailed descriptions, diagrams, and models for the design deliverables. Business analysts and designers, in whom I have confidence, were intimately involved in preparing the design deliverables. Based on their opinions and my review, the design is credible to me. The design is reasonable to the project steering committee members. A low-risk product design[1]:

1. Covers all requirements evenly
2. Describes each component design with a description, diagrams, and models as appropriate

---

[1] The challenge of product design is to carefully make the many required tradeoffs among schedule, functionality or scope, and cost.

3. Emphasizes describing the design and avoids detailing the previously accepted requirements further
4. Responds to both functional and nonfunctional requirements

> Often, project sponsors cannot be close enough to project details to know if the design is comprehensive. Ask experienced business staff not part of the team to review the overall design and offer an independent assessment.

High-Risk Description

The product designs are incomplete, unclear, and not acceptable to me. High-risk design deliverables often exhibit one or more of these characteristics:

1. Cursory design descriptions
2. Uneven detail in the product requirements
3. Lack of team consensus on the scope and design of some deliverables
4. Focus on either functional or nonfunctional requirements to the exclusion of the other

Actions to Address High-Risk Observations

Ask your project manager to lead the team to elaborate on the design deliverables and fill in the gaps. Make sure the right SMEs participate in this discussion. It might be that the design wasn't sufficient because the team didn't have the right expertise. If you see yourself inviting a lot of SMEs beyond the project team to this meeting, it's time to evaluate if you need to add expertise to your team.

Achieving a consensus on design is often tricky. The discussion will spawn various issues and alternatives that require investigation and analysis. The analysis will become the basis for the following:

1. Conclusions about functionality and performance tradeoffs that the team will document in the design deliverables
2. Project scope clarifications
3. Recommendations to resolve business issues requiring the project sponsor's and other stakeholders' approval

As the project sponsor, you must help the team if design questions cannot be settled. You also need to defend the overall design approach to other stakeholders who might have different opinions once it is decided within the team. Ensure the team has the resources to complete the design deliverables thoroughly.

Is the Project Change Management Process Working?

Scope changes will happen. You need an approach for how you will manage proposed changes.

Project change management is the process of managing proposed changes to the project scope.

Topic	Low-risk observations	High-risk observations
Project change management	I've seen a significant list of possible scope additions. But they remain on the list and have not been adopted into the project scope. The project manager rarely recommends scope changes to the project steering committee and me.	I've seen the project manager frequently discuss good ideas that the team adds to the project scope. On multiple occasions, the project manager has recommended scope changes to the project steering committee and me.
PMBOK References	Sixth edition: 4.6, Figure 4-12, 5.2,	Seventh edition: 4.2.4

Low-Risk Description

The team recognizes that their understanding of the project scope will improve as they conduct requirements gathering and design work. The team regularly adds good ideas to a repository of possible scope additions for future projects using the change request[2] form. The project manager rarely proposes scope changes to me. The project steering committee and I approve the rare, proposed changes.

For example, when I challenge the project manager about the surprising lack of project scope changes, they indicate that almost none of

---

[2] See the Glossary entry for Change request.

the proposed scope additions is required to complete the project scope successfully.

It may seem counterintuitive that a good management practice involves *not* adding worthwhile ideas to the project scope. Many projects fail because of such good intentions. Focusing determinedly on the original scope will help your project deliver on time and within budget. That success builds credibility for you and the team. Finishing late, even when caused by good intentions, undermines credibility.

Save these good ideas for future projects. Continuous improvement helps your business succeed, but these ideas are best addressed in future projects.

High-Risk Description

Paradoxically, change control is out of control. Team members are not supporting the project manager's efforts to defend the project scope. High-risk project change management examples include the following:

1. I've become aware that the project manager has approved scope additions without discussing the additions with me.
2. The project manager frequently talks to me and others about the team's good ideas to add to the project scope. This situation indicates a lack of project scope management and a lack of leadership on the project manager's part.
3. The project manager frequently recommends scope additions to me. This situation indicates a well-meaning but inexperienced project manager who fails to recognize that adding project scope dramatically increases the risk that the project will be completed late and over budget.

For example, the project manager has proposed adding more insulation to the warehouse's walls without providing a benefit calculation for energy saving or noise-dampening.

Actions to Address High-Risk Observations

Ask your project manager to explain why they approved project changes. Sincerely listen to your project manager. This conversation will reveal analysis and process gaps that finalized the scope and requirements during project planning. You might also uncover issues with team management and communication. Once you understand the origin and purpose of these changes, explain the following:

1. Downstream effects of constant scope changes on budget and schedule
2. Risk of project cancelation as scope increases

It's tempting to go into this meeting with your project manager and start with the downstream effects. This challenge can demoralize the project manager, who wants to meet end-user needs and feels these changes add value.

After this conversation, help your project manager:

1. Implement a project change management process. If one doesn't exist for this project or your organization, you will need to spend some time developing one. You can use it for all future projects.
2. Remind the team that project scope additions require formal approval from the project manager, project sponsor, and steering committee.

Managing project change control always calls for difficult tradeoffs.[3] Projects that minimize accepting proposed changes are more successful.

Is the Team Overallocated?

Team allocation describes how the team members are assigned to the project tasks. Team overallocation occurs when the effort associated with assigned tasks exceeds team capacity.

---

[3] Read Appendix I—Triple Constraint for more detail about tradeoffs.

Topic	Low-risk observations	High-risk observations
Team allocation	I've seen the team assignments to tasks and believe them reasonable.	I've not seen the team assignments to tasks. I'm concerned that some team members are overallocated and some are underallocated.
PMBOK references	Sixth edition:9.6	Seventh edition: 3.2

Low-Risk Description

I observe the team consistently meeting task completion dates with reasonable quality. The team is happy. No team member is assigned to project tasks for more than 90 percent of their available time on the detailed project plan. Few team members are underallocated.

Shouldn't team members be assigned 100 percent of their availability? Aren't I leaving money on the table if I don't fully allocate them? These are common questions to the 85–90 percent allocation recommendation. Assigning team members 100 percent doesn't leave any cushion when it turns out some tasks have been underestimated. It also leaves no time for training and development, team-building activities, or personal appointments. Giving team members room to breathe will enhance their productivity and contribute to meeting the project schedule.

High-Risk Description

Team allocation to tasks seems to vary widely. High-risk team allocation examples include the following:

1. I observe the team missing completion dates regularly and complaining of being overworked.
2. Everyone rushes around the office in complete silence.
3. It's not clear to me what everyone's current workload is.
4. There isn't much collaboration because no one has the time for that.

Actions to Address High-Risk Observations

The only way to reasonably distribute work and know who is over-allocated is to assign a team member to every task and create effort estimates for every task. It may seem tedious or bureaucratic, but it has enormous value. With this data in hand, your project manager can then meet with the team to discuss who is overallocated or underallocated and reassign some tasks to achieve workload balance. Your team will thank you.

Once the estimates are complete, the typical result is that every team member is overallocated. At this point, your project manager will likely need your assistance to approve an increased budget to bring on more team members and your political power to assign the right people. Flex your muscles to acquire the right people for your project.

If your team has been overallocated for most of the project, nudge the project manager to recognize the extra effort through sports tickets, days off, or a cash bonus. Something more than a $5 gift card to Starbucks.

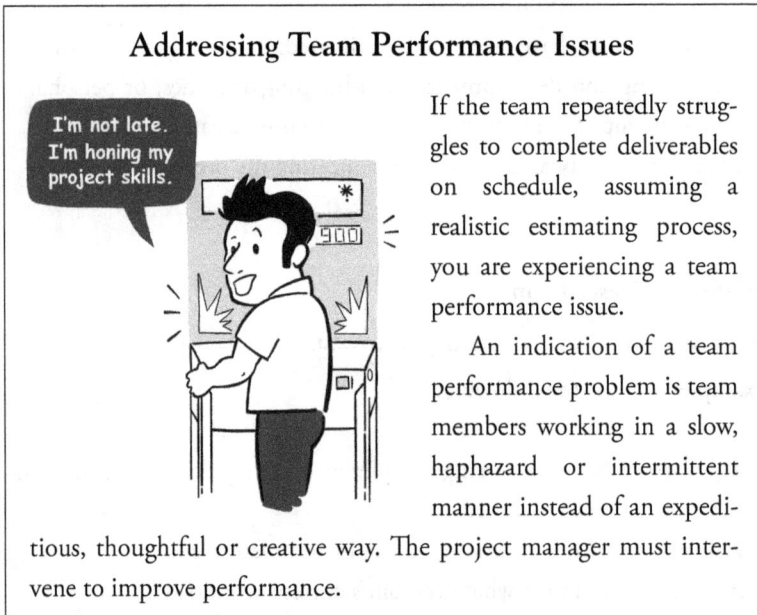

Addressing Team Performance Issues

I'm not late. I'm honing my project skills.

If the team repeatedly struggles to complete deliverables on schedule, assuming a realistic estimating process, you are experiencing a team performance issue.

An indication of a team performance problem is team members working in a slow, haphazard or intermittent manner instead of an expeditious, thoughtful or creative way. The project manager must intervene to improve performance.

Figure 8.2 Team member honing critical skills

Is Project Progress Perceptible?

Project progress shows how well or poorly the project is moving toward completion. Project progress tracking uses metrics[4] to show which deliverables are underway and how well the team is progressing.

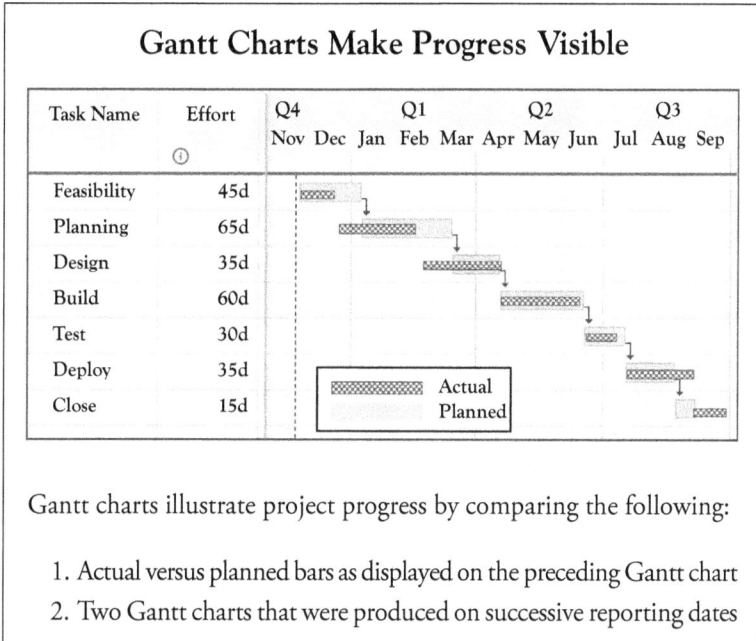

Gantt Charts Make Progress Visible

Task Name	Effort	Q4		Q1		Q2		Q3	
	ⓘ	Nov Dec	Jan Feb Mar	Apr May Jun	Jul Aug Sep				
Feasibility	45d								
Planning	65d								
Design	35d								
Build	60d								
Test	30d								
Deploy	35d								
Close	15d								

Legend: Actual / Planned

Gantt charts illustrate project progress by comparing the following:

1. Actual versus planned bars as displayed on the preceding Gantt chart
2. Two Gantt charts that were produced on successive reporting dates

Figure 8.3 Project Gantt chart

Topic	Low-risk observations	High-risk observations
Project progress	I've seen the same summary Gantt chart illustrating reasonable project progress on multiple occasions. I've seen metrics such as percent complete, effort-to-date, or effort remaining to know which deliverables are underway. Deliverables are completed on time more often than not.	I've never seen a Gantt chart. Successive Gantt charts show little or no progress. I'm simply *hoping* to see a completed deliverable by the due date. I've not seen metrics. Deliverables are often late. My team feels frazzled.
PMBOK references	Sixth edition: 6.5.3.2	Seventh edition: 2.4.8, 2.7.2.2, 2.7.2.5

---

[4] See the Glossary entry for Metric.

Low-Risk Description

I see the same Gantt chart updated at every steering committee meeting to show progress for the in-progress deliverables relative to the project plan. One or more regularly updated metrics measure progress on every in-progress deliverable. I can see which deliverables are on time, at risk, and late. I see that the project is making steady progress.

I've heard the project manager and the team summarize the project's progress in a few sentences.

High-Risk Description

I can't confidently see progress on the Gantt charts I'm shown. High-risk project progress examples include the following:

1. The list of deliverables and expected completion dates constantly changes when comparing this month's Gantt chart with last month's.
2. I've observed that work on deliverables is often incomplete and late. Task effort estimates may be too optimistic.
3. The project manager and team are unable to summarize the project's progress. There are lots of excuses.
4. The entire project is forecast to complete well after the planned completion date.
5. The team complains of being overworked.
6. Everyone rushes around the office in complete silence.
7. I've seen few metrics for understanding work-in-progress or labeling deliverables as complete. This situation leads to debates about whether a deliverable has met its objectives, is falling behind, or is complete as there is no way to determine status or completion.

Actions to Address High-Risk Observations

Ask your project manager to describe the reasons for the apparent lack of project progress. Make sure you *listen* to what they are saying. You will learn important things about your project and team. When your project manager brings you problems, it's also essential that you don't immediately freak out and start assigning blame.

What can you do to help achieve a reliable project schedule? Is your project manager being held to some overly optimistic deadline imposed by someone outside the project? Does your team include the right people for the deliverables?

Sometimes it's helpful to reestimate the balance of the project. Instruct your project manager and team to reestimate the remaining work of the project. Often, difficulties with deliverable completion are the consequence of a poorly planned project. The replanning will result in the following:

1. Higher effort estimates that are more realistic.
2. Assignment of tasks that previously didn't have an assigned team member.
3. The addition of new tasks that were missed in the original detailed project plan.
4. A better understanding of deliverable precedence.
5. An unavoidable higher project cost estimate. If the cost stays the same or goes down through replanning, you have a problem in the estimating process.
6. A revised project completion date that is later but more realistic.

Results #5 and #6 will need your support to achieve approval from the project steering committee. It would be best to approach the steering committee with objective data about missed project tasks and overall project delay.

Yearning for Project Progress

Project sponsors often struggle to observe project progress.

Sometimes the lack of issue resolution causes the team to slow down, waiting for direction from the project sponsor or other stakeholders. The project manager needs to show more leadership by proceeding assumptively. The team must continue its work expecting that stakeholders will formally accept its recommendations for resolving issues eventually.

(Continues)

(*Continued*)

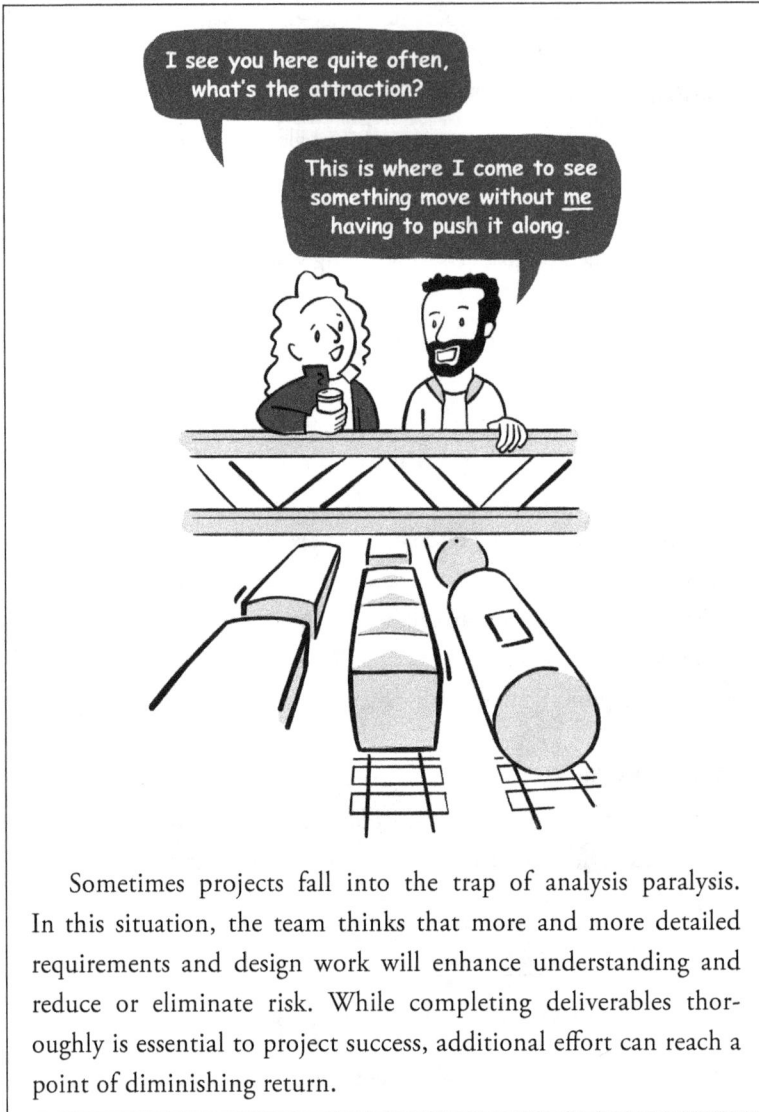

Sometimes projects fall into the trap of analysis paralysis. In this situation, the team thinks that more and more detailed requirements and design work will enhance understanding and reduce or eliminate risk. While completing deliverables thoroughly is essential to project success, additional effort can reach a point of diminishing return.

Figure 8.4 Watching railcars moving at the railyard

Are Progress Metrics Available for Deliverables?

The most common metric for measuring progress is the percent complete of every deliverable and your entire project. However, don't just focus on the percent complete.

Topic	Low-risk observations	High-risk observations
Percent complete	Percent complete is one of multiple metrics reported to me and used to determine that my project is on schedule.	I observe percent complete is often optimistically overstated. Percent complete is the only metric reported to me to determine if my project is on schedule.
PMBOK references	Sixth edition: 7.1.3.1	Seventh edition: 2.7.2.7

Figure 8.5 *Project progress metrics*

Low-Risk Description

My organization uses multiple metrics to assess project status. Example metrics include the following:

1. Percent complete variance against schedule
2. Expenditure variance against budget
3. Effort variance against estimate
4. Earned value analysis

I'm confident that the metrics reported are reasonably accurate.

High-Risk Description

Percent complete estimation is wildly optimistic. High-risk percent complete examples include the following:

1. I'm not confident the percentages complete reported are reasonably accurate.
2. I've observed multiple project deliverables sitting at 80–90 percent complete for weeks or even months. In this situation, percent complete isn't telling me the whole story.
3. Percent complete is the sole focus of steering committee or project team meetings.

Actions to Address High-Risk Observations

Anyone undertaking a home renovation project understands that percent complete can be a misleading metric. You do most of the work, like installing new carpet, painting the walls, and installing new doors on two weekends. But it takes you another month to install the new door handles to finish the project. Similarly, many projects linger in this 85–99 percent complete status for too long.

While percent complete is a common and valuable metric, it can convey an overly optimistic sense of accomplishment when not tracked alongside other metrics.

Without organization-defined metrics, your team needs to develop a few metrics for project status and success. Typical metrics include the following:

1. Forecasted completion date
2. Forecasted cost at completion
3. Forecasted effort at completion
4. Number of deficiencies resolved per week

It's worth evaluating the formulas associated with earned value management (EVM). A Google search can tell you all about these. These metrics are becoming more popular in our data-heavy society. Evaluate the formulas and determine which will add value to your project and organization. Using all of them for your project will be overkill.

Share the results with your organization's executive leadership team once your team has run a successful project with some of the aforementioned metrics. Suggest that all the organization's projects use similar metrics where applicable. That way, the performance of all projects can be compared apples to apples across your organization!

It's easy for teams to become overoptimistic and overstate the percent complete of tasks. Encourage realistic self-assessment of the remaining work.

View all percent complete metrics with a grain of salt.

Does the Team Mitigate Risks?

Risk mitigation involves planning and performing tasks to mitigate high-likelihood and high-impact risks.

Topic	Low-risk observations	High-risk observations
Risk mitigation	I've seen risk mitigation tasks that appear comprehensive. I've observed the team performing risk mitigation tasks.	I've not seen the team planning risk mitigation tasks. The team is not performing risk mitigation tasks.
PMBOK references	Sixth edition: 11.5, 11.6	Seventh edition: 3.10

Low-Risk Description

I've seen risk mitigation tasks in the detailed project plan for high-likelihood and high-impact risks that appear reasonably comprehensive.

I've observed the team performing risk mitigation tasks for high-likelihood and high-impact risks. I believe such preemptive work is helpful to avoid these risks turning into an expensive reality that will also delay the project.

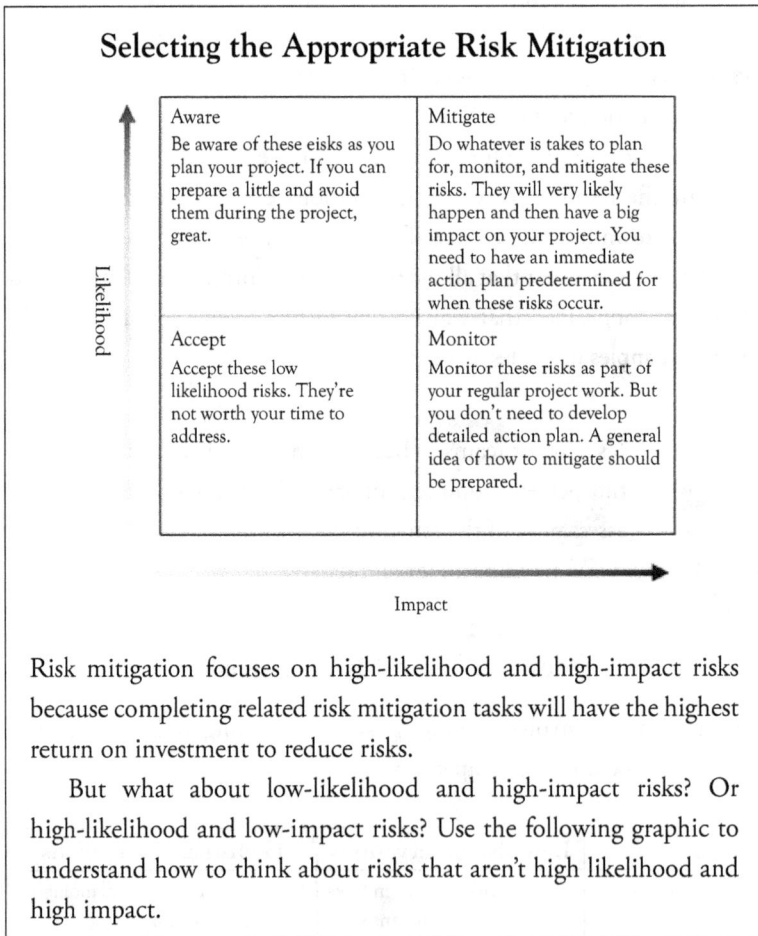

Selecting the Appropriate Risk Mitigation

Likelihood ↑		
	Aware — Be aware of these eisks as you plan your project. If you can prepare a little and avoid them during the project, great.	**Mitigate** — Do whatever is takes to plan for, monitor, and mitigate these risks. They will very likely happen and then have a big impact on your project. You need to have an immediate action plan predetermined for when these risks occur.
	Accept — Accept these low likelihood risks. They're not worth your time to address.	**Monitor** — Monitor these risks as part of your regular project work. But you don't need to develop detailed action plan. A general idea of how to mitigate should be prepared.

Impact →

Risk mitigation focuses on high-likelihood and high-impact risks because completing related risk mitigation tasks will have the highest return on investment to reduce risks.

But what about low-likelihood and high-impact risks? Or high-likelihood and low-impact risks? Use the following graphic to understand how to think about risks that aren't high likelihood and high impact.

Figure 8.6 Paying attention to risk mitigation

High-Risk Description

I've not seen the team concerned about mitigating high-likelihood and high-impact risks. High-risk risk mitigation examples include the following:

1. The team is hoping that ignoring risks will cause them to fade away.
2. The team is aware of risks but keeps deferring mitigation tasks.
3. The team is not performing risk mitigation tasks.

Actions to Address High-Risk Observations

Ask your project manager to increase the priority of mitigating high-likelihood and high-impact risks. While performing risk mitigation tasks is likely to create a schedule delay, this delay is a small fraction of the delay that occurs when risks turn into reality.

Does the Project Schedule Contain Meaningful Milestones?

Milestones are the essential points or events that occur along your project schedule.

Topic	Low-risk observations	High-risk observations
Project milestones	The project schedule includes essential milestones. The milestone dates I've seen seem realistic and are met more often than not.	The project schedule includes a few milestones. The milestone dates I've seen are often padded, infrequently met, or unknown to the team.
PMBOK references	Sixth edition: 6.2.3.3	Seventh edition: Figure 2-12

Low-Risk Description

The project milestones and associated dates appear reasonable to me. The milestone dates are frequently achieved.

The number of milestones is roughly proportional to the size of the project. Small projects can be well defined with few milestones, while large projects require more milestones. Each phase of the project typically contains at least two milestones. Examples of project milestones could be the following:

1. Finished framing the building under construction
2. Finished testing the software in the test environment
3. Every actor has all their lines memorized for the play
4. Completed data gathering from prototype testing

High-Risk Description

The defined milestones vary considerably in importance to the project. High-risk milestone examples include the following:

1. There are no milestones shown in the project schedule that I've seen.
2. I see milestones in the project schedule, but their position doesn't make sense.
3. There are many milestones at the start of the project and few at the end, or vice versa.
4. The planned milestone dates are not achieved often.

Actions to Address High-Risk Observations

Ask your project manager to work with the team to develop a reasonable set of project milestones. Ensure milestones are distributed throughout every phase of the project schedule.

When your team successfully meets project milestones, you need to recognize their excellent work. Hold a celebratory lunch or take the team out for a fun activity. This action will communicate to the team that you acknowledge their work.

Ensure your team fills out the lessons learned register before moving on to the next phase. It can be tempting to say you'll fill out the lessons learned register at the end of the project, but you will have forgotten many items when it finishes.

When you've completed a milestone, make sure your team takes a breath to celebrate successes and review shortcomings. Don't just steamroll into the next phase of the project.

Is Project Communication Occurring Regularly?

Communication is about performing the tasks listed in the communication management plan throughout the project's life.

Topic	Low-risk observations	High-risk observations
Project communi-cation	I've seen a communication plan. I know who is responsible for project communication with stakeholders and team members. I've seen well-designed communication artifacts. I've seen communication occurring.	I haven't seen a communication plan. I don't know who is responsible for project communication. Communication happens ad hoc and typically in response to stakeholder requests for a status update. Communication artifacts contain contradictory information.
PMBOK references	Sixth edition:10.1, 10.1.3.1	Seventh edition: 2.4.4, 2.5.4

Low-Risk Description

I've seen a single document that describes the communication plan. It looks comprehensive to me. The plan includes the following:

1. A summary of the planned communication approach based on stakeholder needs
2. Who is responsible for communication with which stakeholders
3. A schedule of communication events targeting the various stakeholders
4. The planned data gathering to gauge communication effectiveness

Regular communication using various channels is evident. Awareness of the project is widespread. Communication includes project status and progress against milestones.

High-Risk Description

I observe sporadic and confusing communication. High-risk communication situations include the following:

1. The written communication plan I've seen is incomplete.
2. I wonder who is responsible for project communication.
3. Communication happens at random intervals whenever a team member *feels* like communicating something.
4. Various team members have expressed contradictory descriptions of the project.
5. I see the person responsible is not performing adequately.
6. I observe that awareness of the project is uneven.
7. Communication artifacts are poorly designed, contain contradictory information, and are published irregularly.
8. Some stakeholders have made inaccurate statements about the project.

The invisible project manager. Some project managers are more comfortable devoting their time to the tactical minutiae of managing the project. The job description of project managers includes communicating up and out. Project sponsors sometimes need to remind project managers of this aspect of their role. For more information on this point, please read "How to be a winning project manager: Manage up and out" at this link: www.jocelynlapointe.com/resources.

Actions to Address High-Risk Observations

Ask your project manager to meet with the team to review the following:

1. Adequacy of the communication plan
2. Sufficiency of the communication execution

The conclusions from this discussion will be the basis of your improved communication work. Ensure that the person responsible for project communication has the time and aptitude for this job. If you or the project manager are not confident in the person's ability, make a change.

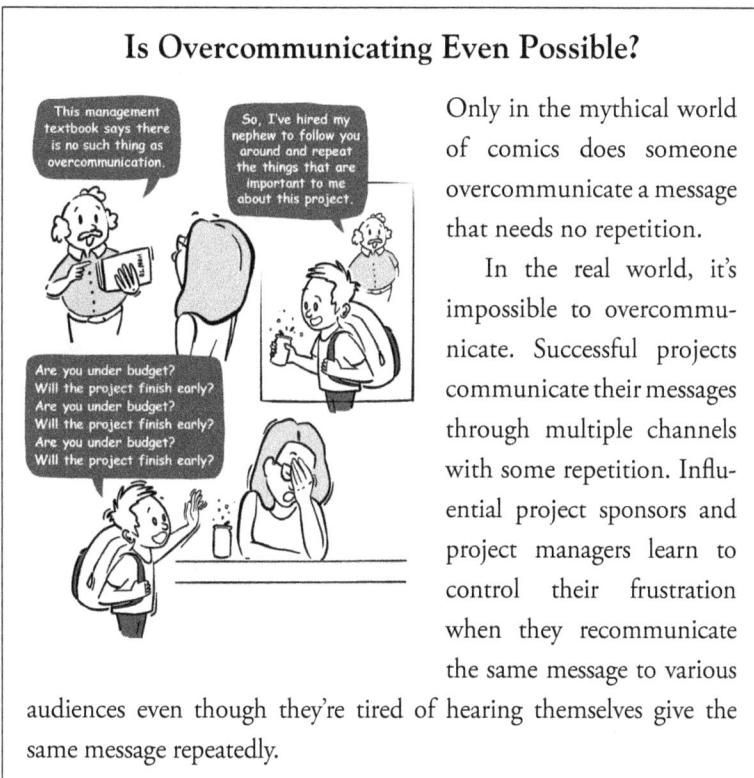

Is Overcommunicating Even Possible?

Only in the mythical world of comics does someone overcommunicate a message that needs no repetition.

In the real world, it's impossible to overcommunicate. Successful projects communicate their messages through multiple channels with some repetition. Influential project sponsors and project managers learn to control their frustration when they recommunicate the same message to various audiences even though they're tired of hearing themselves give the same message repeatedly.

Figure 8.7 Effective projects overcommunicate

Are Project Expenditure Updates Reported?

Project expenditures are the total costs incurred and committed so far to advance the project.

Topic	Low-risk observations	High-risk observations
Project expenditures	I receive regular updates on project expenditures. The cumulative expenditure amounts by line item seem plausible to me.	I rarely receive updates on project expenditures. The cumulative expenditure amounts by line item I see vary significantly over time.
PMBOK references	Sixth edition: 3.13, 7.4	Seventh edition: 2.4.2.4, 2.7.2.7, Figure 2-26

Low-Risk Description

The regular project expenditure report seems plausible to the project steering committee members and me in the context of the current project status. A low-risk project expenditure report includes the following elements:

1. Cumulative expenditure-to-date amounts by line item[5]
2. Budget amounts by line item
3. Expenditure variance against budget amounts
4. A few notes that explain the highlights and surprising variances

High-Risk Description

The variations in the project expenditures from report to report don't seem plausible to me. A high-risk project expenditure report exhibits some of the following characteristics:

1. Incomplete cumulative expenditure-to-date amounts by line item
2. Budget line item amounts that change from one report to the next

---

[5] Be restrained about asking the project manager for detailed expenditure or variance reports by deliverable, phase, or breakdowns within high-level budget line items. Such requests create a lot of administrative work for little benefit to the project.

3. Expenditure variances against budget line item amounts change significantly from report to report

4. The number of budget line items varies from one report to the next

Actions to Address High-Risk Observations

Consult your organization's process assets. Some organizations already have a policy[6] in place for project expenditure reporting. If your project manager is not following them, review the policy with your project manager. It could simply be that your project manager wasn't aware of the policy.

If your organization doesn't have one, direct your project manager to lead the team to develop a more consistent expenditure reporting process. Review the process with the project manager to ensure it includes your organization's financial KPIs. Bring this policy to your executive leadership team and suggest it for organizationwide implementation. You could be a hero for developing an approach that helps other projects.

Sometimes project expenditure reports are misleading because they show understated amounts due to incurred costs that the vendor has not yet invoiced. You can recognize misleading reports when the month-to-month increase in expenditures is lower than your rough guess. Correct this problem by ensuring project expenditure reports include estimates for such incurred costs.[7]

---

[6] See the Glossary entry for Business policy.

[7] In some organizations, the calculation of project expenditures results in time-consuming reconciliation tasks to explain differences among cash accounting, accrual accounting, and project accounting. Stick to cash accounting if possible. In the end, projects are valued for their deliverables, not how well they addressed financial reporting quirks.

Are Project Expenditure Forecasts Plausible?

The expenditure forecast is the sum of project expenditures incurred to date plus a forecast of estimated expenditures required to complete the project.

Topic	Low-risk observations	High-risk observations
Project expenditure forecast	I receive regular project expenditure forecasts. The expenditure forecast amounts by line item seem plausible to me.	I don't receive expenditure forecasts. The expenditure forecast amounts I see vary considerably from one reporting period to the next.
PMBOK references	Sixth edition: 9.6	Seventh edition: Figure 2-31, 2.7.2.7

Low-Risk Description

The regular project expenditure forecasts seem reasonable to the project steering committee members and me based on the current project status. A low-risk project expenditure forecast includes the following elements:

1. Cumulative expenditure to date amounts by line item
2. Estimate-to-complete amounts for every line item
3. Budget line item amounts
4. Expenditure variances at completion against budget line item amounts
5. A few notes that explain the highlights

High-Risk Description

The significant variations in the project expenditure forecasts from report to report don't seem plausible to me. A high-risk project expenditure forecast exhibits some of these characteristics:

1. Incomplete cumulative expenditure to date amounts
2. Incomplete estimate-to-complete amounts
3. The forecast amounts are simply the unspent budget line item amounts

4. Budget line item amounts change from one report to the next
5. Expenditure variance at completion against budget line-item amounts change significantly from one report to the following one
6. Expenditure variance at completion against budget is trending materially over budget

Actions to Address High-Risk Observations

While some organizations already have a policy for project expenditure reporting, few have one for forecasts. If you are part of a lucky organization with a forecasting process and your project manager is not following it, review it with your project manager. It could simply be that your project manager isn't aware of the policy because having one is rare.

If your organization doesn't have a policy, direct your project manager to lead the team to develop a more consistent expenditure forecasting process. Review the process with the project manager to ensure it has your organization's correct forecast KPIs. Bring this policy to your executive leadership team and suggest it be implemented organization-wide. You could be a hero for developing an approach that helps other projects.

If the expenditure variance at completion against budget is trending materially over budget, there are only two difficult actions to consider:

1. Reduce scope. This action means the project will achieve only part of the goal.
2. Increase the budget. This action means the business case for the project becomes less attractive.

Project expenditure forecasts are prone to overly optimistic estimates. This underestimation will produce a rosy but unlikely project completion date and project cost at completion. You can recognize this optimism when the month-to-month increase in percentage complete increases rapidly initially and then slows to a crawl as the project progresses.

Is the Team Environment Respectful?

A respectful team environment is crucial for morale, collaboration, and productivity.

Topic	Low-risk observations	High-risk observations
Team environment	I've observed the team interacting respectfully and collaborating well.	I've observed tensions in team conversations. I've observed the project manager treating some team members better than others. I've observed conflict and arguments among team members.
PMBOK references	Sixth edition: 9.4	Seventh edition: 3.2

Low-Risk Description

I've observed the team members regularly interacting respectfully and collaborating well. The team listens to other points of view and reaches a consensus on issues.

High-Risk Description

I'm astonished by the lack of respect with which team members treat each other. A high-risk team environment exhibits some of these unacceptable behaviors that undermine team effectiveness:

1. Sarcastic or inappropriately critical comments
2. Bullying of some team members by others
3. Misogynistic attitudes and comments
4. Swearing
5. Racist and ethnic slurs

Actions to Address High-Risk Observations

Direct the project manager to remind team members to behave respectfully. The project manager must:

1. Set an excellent example with positive and encouraging comments.
2. Immediately challenge unacceptable behavior when it occurs.

3. Formally reprimand team members in private.

4. Remove team members from the team that don't or won't improve their behavior. No one's expertise is sufficient to be exempted from this standard of conduct.

That Deliverable Will Cost How Much?

Yogi, Jocelyn, and Aunt Gisela once rented electric bikes to ride around Vienna, Austria. The e-bikes required a €500 deposit each. Due to some constraints, the only credit card at hand that could be used at the bike dealer in Vienna was the card that sent automatic alerts for every transaction. These automatic alerts went straight to Yogi's wife, Connie, in Canada. After Jocelyn charges over €1,500 to the card, she immediately receives a panicky e-mail from Connie asking why on earth we've spent €1,500 at some bike shop in Vienna. Once Yogi and Jocelyn explain that most of that amount is the deposit on the e-bikes, Connie calms down and goes back to sleep.

Understanding your overall project cost is essential, but knowing when and where those funds will be spent is important. Connie wouldn't have blinked if we'd spent that sum on airplane tickets, but a bike shop was utterly unexpected.

(Continues)

(*Continued*)

> Managing your project budget is the same. The project steering committee wouldn't have a problem with a significant upfront expenditure such as a large piece of machinery clearly shown in the budget. But the steering committee would hit the roof if you spent a similar or even lower amount of money on a fancy imported cappuccino machine for the team.
>
> You need to be clear about what, when, and the purpose of your expenditures, especially if they represent a large portion of the project budget.

Figure 8.8 *Spending money for project-related services*

Summary

The purpose of the build phase is to build the deliverables specified in the design.

The most common build problems include the following:

1. Inferior quality caused by schedule pressure
2. Overoptimistic status reporting

CHAPTER 9

Test

Overview

Test is the project phase consisting of quality assurance (QA) tasks and acceptance testing by the team and the client.

Organizations sometimes confuse or conflate quality control (QC) and QA.

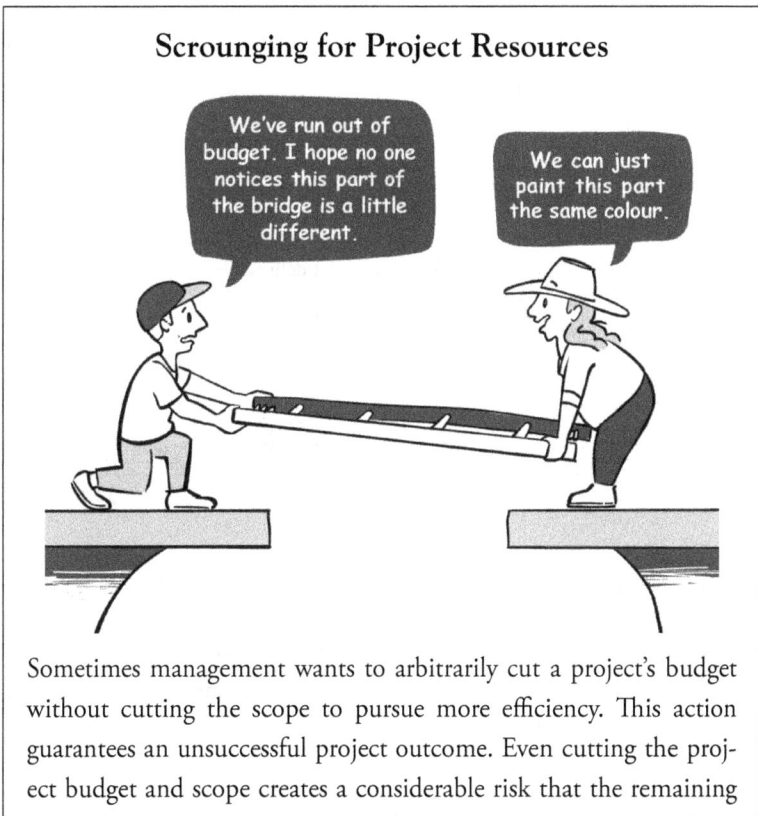

Scrounging for Project Resources

We've run out of budget. I hope no one notices this part of the bridge is a little different.

We can just paint this part the same colour.

Sometimes management wants to arbitrarily cut a project's budget without cutting the scope to pursue more efficiency. This action guarantees an unsuccessful project outcome. Even cutting the project budget and scope creates a considerable risk that the remaining

(Continues)

(*Continued*)

> budget won't deliver a net benefit. It's often better to cancel projects than to cut budgets.
>
> On the other hand, projects can always produce more results and quality with more resources. Knowing what is fit for purpose is frequently a complex challenge for project teams. In our world, where companies operate around the clock and around the globe, high-quality project deliverables are essential. They are not a nice-to-have. Be careful when you propose a project budget cut.

Figure 9.1 Setting an appropriate project budget

Do Acceptance Criteria for Deliverables Exist?

Acceptance criteria[1] ensure that deliverables meet the requirements and the design specifications.

Topic	Low-risk observations	High-risk observations
Acceptance criteria	I've seen a reasonable list of essential criteria that must be met to ensure deliverable acceptance. Most of the acceptance criteria include numeric values.	Various descriptions with no numeric criteria define the deliverable acceptance criteria I've seen. Deliverable acceptance is based on someone's gut feeling. Deliverable acceptance is based on the opinion of the person assigned to complete the deliverable.
PMBOK references	Sixth edition: 5.3.3.1	Seventh edition: 3.8, 2.6.2.1, 2.6.2.2

Low-Risk Description

I've seen a bulleted list of acceptance criteria for every deliverable. The team understands the criteria. The team can measure most of the

---

[1] See the Glossary entry for Acceptance criteria.

criteria objectively. Examples of low-risk acceptance criteria include the following:

1. The maximum variation in weight of the product is 0.05 ml.
2. A watertight windshield must be installed on every vehicle leaving the assembly line.
3. The system can handle 100 simultaneous active end-users with a response time of 10 seconds or less.

High-Risk Description

The acceptance criteria are vaguely defined or not easily understood by me. Acceptance criteria that include vague phrases like best, easy-to-use, and industry-leading are not helpful because the team cannot measure them. Examples of high-risk acceptance criteria include the following:

1. Up to eight cans of the product must fit into the cardboard shipping box.
2. Our organization will provide the best shopping experience for the whole family on our e-commerce website.
3. The building cannot sway too much on a windy day.

Actions to Address High-Risk Observations

If the acceptance criteria are undefined or vaguely defined, you must fix that quickly before the project proceeds too far. Ask your project manager to meet with the team and rework the acceptance criteria for every deliverable. Frame the acceptance criteria as close to the SMART[2] concept as possible. Communicate where the team can find the acceptance criteria and ensure they are referenced during subsequent work.

Once the project team has defined the project acceptance criteria, call on a few SMEs in your organization to double-check that those are the

---

[2] SMART is an acronym that stands for Specific, Measurable, Achievable, Realistic, and Timely.

appropriate acceptance criteria. Getting the acceptance criteria right at the beginning of your project or as close to the beginning as possible will save you a big headache as you try to finish the project.

Formulating acceptance criteria often triggers reviewing your project scope statement and various project assumptions in the project charter. If changes to those documents are needed, instruct your project manager to submit change orders ASAP.

> Good acceptance criteria communicate project priorities, simplify scope validation, and ensure deliverable acceptance. Together these definitions avoid unhappy surprises about project requirements at the end of the project.

Are QC Tasks Being Performed?

The QC[3] tasks ensure the quality of your project deliverables. QC is preemptive work to reduce or avoid defects.

Topic	Low-risk observations	High-risk observations
QC	I've seen a satisfactory QC plan for the project. I've seen evidence of QC work.	I'm not aware of any QC plan for the project. I haven't seen evidence of QC work.
PMBOK references	Sixth edition: 8.3.3.1	Seventh edition: 2.6.3, 3.8

Low-Risk Description

Low-risk QC looks like this:

1. I've seen the QC plan in our organization's documents.
2. The team understands how to implement it for the project. The team members know what aspects of their work contribute to overall project quality.
3. Their work doesn't fail QC often. When deliverables fail, there are processes to correct failures and ensure they are not repeated.

---

[3] See the Glossary entry for Quality control.

Larger organizations typically assign a quality department/person to the project. They lead QC work.

> Many people feel like they can skip the QC process if they perform a robust QA procedure later. Skipping QC will just drag out the QA process, and there will be significantly more waste and rework. Don't be tempted to skip!

High-Risk Description

QC is out of control. High-risk QC examples include:

1. I've observed that work on deliverables is monitored haphazardly with no standardization across deliverables.
2. Team members monitoring deliverable quality rely on gut feelings of goodness rather than metrics and facts.
3. Project deliverables often fail the QC procedure.[4] This outcome adds significant effort to the project for rework.
4. I've not observed a process for implementing corrective or preventive action.

Actions to Address High-Risk Observations

Intervene immediately to stop more shoddy work from continuing. Ask your project manager to address issues affecting quality with the team. Make every effort to attend this meeting to provide visible support to the project manager. Your team will likely push back when you question the quality of their work. Bring all the data you can about rework and QC procedure failures. Tell them that project work is on hold until they can develop and implement a QC plan.

Ask your project manager to enlist the quality department to develop a QC plan for your project's deliverables. If those resources are unavailable, hire a consultant to work with the team to create a QC plan. Start

---

[4] See the Glossary entry for Business procedure.

with a root–cause analysis of QC failures. Once you've discovered your root causes, implement corrective action. Ensure your team agrees to an improved process so that the same mistakes don't pop up again.

Your team should participate from day one in creating the QC plan. They will be the ones to implement it and learn what a quality deliverable looks like. A Google search about QC plans can also be helpful. Once a QC plan has been developed, ensure it's applied to all the project work.

When you perform QC, you will discover more errors and institute fixes that contribute to improved quality. More broadly, you will create a project culture that plans quality into its work. Planning and careful work produce quality deliverables. Quality cannot be inspected into existence.

Achieving Quality Shapes for Peppers Is Not Easy

Only one of four accepted quality shapes can be produced when cutting peppers in the Schulz household:

1. Short and fat for use in a green salad or grilling
2. Long and skinny for stir-fries
3. Long and chunky for eating raw or dipping into hummus
4. Diced as an added ingredient in soups or stews

Before anyone dares cut a pepper in the Schulz home, we must first understand what shape the head chef expects. Then, once she confirms the desired shape, we prepare a small sample for the head chef to inspect for conformity.

This routine is a perfect example of quality management. The team first agrees upon the requirement (pepper shape), then, after a bit of execution, there is an inspection to confirm acceptable quality. All your project deliverables should utilize this quality management process.

Figure 9.2 Deliverable quality management

Are QA Tasks Being Performed?

The QA[5] tasks verify the quality of deliverables after their completion.

Topic	Low-risk observations	High-risk observations
QA	I've seen a suitable QA plan for the project. I've seen QA reports for our project deliverables.	I'm not aware of any QA plan for the project. I haven't seen QA reports for our project deliverables. The QA reports I've seen for our project deliverables appeared incomplete.
PMBOK references	Sixth edition: Figure 8.1.2, 8.2	Seventh edition: 2.6.3, 3.4.3.1, 3.8

Low-Risk Description

Low-risk QA looks like this:

1. I've seen a comprehensive QA procedure in my organization's documents.
2. The team understands how it applies to the project and how to implement it for the project. The team knows how their deliverables contribute to overall project quality.
3. Few deliverables fail the QA procedure.

In larger organizations, a quality department assigns a person to the project and leads assurance work.

High-Risk Description

QA is not providing me with much assurance. High-risk QA examples include the following:

1. I've observed that project deliverables fail the QA procedure often.
2. There is frequent rework.
3. I've not observed a process for corrective or preventive action.

---

[5] See the Glossary entry for Quality assurance.

Actions to Address High-Risk Observations

Intervene immediately to stop more shoddy work from continuing. Ask your project manager to meet with the team to discuss quality issues. Make every effort to attend this meeting to provide visible support to the project manager. Your team will likely push back when you question their work. Bring all the data you can about rework and QA procedure failures. Tell the team that project work is on hold until they develop and implement a QA plan.

Ask your project manager to enlist the quality department to develop a QA plan for your project's deliverables. If those resources are unavailable, hire a consultant to work with the team to create a QA plan. Start with a root–cause analysis of QA failures. Once you've discovered your root causes, implement corrective action. Ensure your team agrees to an improved process so that the same mistake doesn't happen again.

Your team should participate from day one in creating the QA plan. They will be the ones to implement it and learn what a quality deliverable looks like. A Google search about QA plans can also be helpful. Once a QA plan is developed, ensure your project manager applies it to the project work.

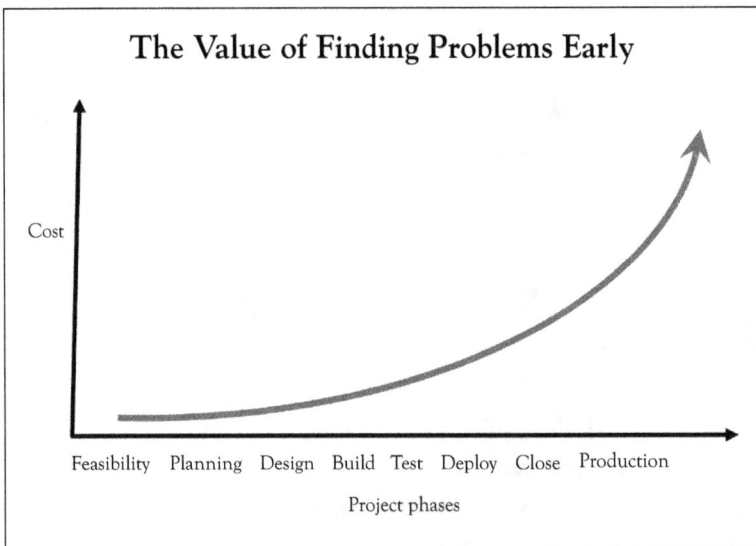

Figure 9.3 How QA tasks reduce project cost

QA can't just happen near the end of a project. Performing QA tasks for major deliverables throughout the life of your project will catch minor problems early on when they are cheaper to fix and before they become big problems, as illustrated by this chart.[6]

Is the Team Experiencing Turnover?

Team turnover is a metric that measures how often people on the team are replaced. High team turnover[7] is a risk to your project.

Topic	Low-risk observations	High-risk observations
Team turnover	Team turnover is low. The team appears happy to be on the project.	Team turnover is surprisingly high. Project morale varies significantly over time.
PMBOK references	Sixth edition: 9.4.3.1, p.310, Trends and emerging practices in project resource management	Seventh edition: 2.7.2.6

Low-Risk Description

Many team members I've met started on the project and are still working on it. Continuity in the team helps us retain essential knowledge about the project. The team seems content to be at work. Low-risk teams exhibit low turnover due to the following:

1. Team expertise and experience are closely aligned with the expectations of project performance.
2. The organization recognizes team achievements.
3. The project manager exhibits reasonable leadership skills.
4. The project work is valuable to the organization and attractive to the team.

---

[6] D. Sobek. October 3, 2014. *Frontloading Product Development.*

[7] High team turnover adds risk through loss of team memory and the cost of recruiting and onboarding new team members.

High-Risk Description

Team turnover is killing morale and project progress. High-risk team turnover examples include the following:

1. I keep seeing new faces.
2. I hear a lot of grumbling or observe strained silences when communicating with the team.
3. There is something awkward in the air when I walk past or talk to the team members. I can cut the tension with a knife.
4. The number of sick days taken and unexplained absences are much larger than on other projects.

The most common sources of high team turnover are:

1. A poor project manager annoys the team with their poor leadership skills.
2. The expectations of project performance are unreasonable.
3. The organization exhibits a culture of assigning blame.
4. Team members believe being associated with the project will harm their reputation and career prospects.
5. The technology choices made are not capable of achieving the project goal.
6. The skills that team members are acquiring make them highly sought-after professionals. As a result, they are being recruited actively.

The number one cause of high team turnover is a poor project manager. Replacing a project manager is never fun. However, procrastinating the awkward decision only allows the problem to add cost and schedule to the project. Taking this action is one of the reasons you're paid the big bucks.

Actions to Address High-Risk Observations

Addressing high team turnover issues requires actions that are uncomfortable for many. However, the alternative of letting a project flounder and eventually be canceled is much worse. Actions you can take as the project sponsor to address high team turnover include:

1. Ask the project manager to work on developing more leadership skills. If that's not feasible or effective, you must replace the project manager.

2. Revise project performance expectations in collaboration with the project manager. The rest of the management team will not receive the likely schedule extension well. It will require your skills to sell reality.

3. Set a tone for yourself that avoids assigning blame. You can encourage the project manager to exhibit the same behavior.

4. Become more visible to the team to communicate that the project is essential and address team morale issues.

5. Ask the project manager to collaborate with the team to update the technology risks if there's a concern that the technology choices are inadequate.

6. Collaborate with the project manager on pay increases and retention bonuses to address headhunting.

Why Would You Put Up With That Behavior?

Jocelyn was in the middle of a baking spree one month when her baking mixture tasted a little funny. At first, she thought it was a problem with poor measurement, but she confirmed her recipe. Then she checked her main ingredients: flour, butter, and sugar. All were in order. It wasn't until she checked her new bottle of vanilla extract that she discovered the problem. The vanilla

(*Continues*)

(*Continued*)

> tasted terrible, and even in the small dash used in baking, it ruined the whole mixture.
>
> A poor-performing team member will cause the same problem. The other team members can work hard like the flour, butter, and sugar, but a small dash of a defective person can ruin your entire project. It's expensive to throw out a whole bottle of vanilla, but keeping it lingering in the cupboard doesn't do anyone any good. Keeping a poor-performing team member is the same. The sooner you terminate them, the better.

Figure 9.4 *Removing toxic team members*

Summary

The purpose of the test phase is to test the deliverables to ensure that they:

1. Comprehensively cover the project's scope
2. Are fit for purpose
3. Meet the quality standard defined for the project

The most common test problems include the following:

1. Superficial testing caused by a cursory test plan, schedule pressure, and insufficient resources
2. A significant number of defects caused by design gaps and lack of quality during the build phase

CHAPTER 10

Deploy

Overview

Deploy is the project phase that places project deliverables into routine use. This phase performs transitional tasks required for sustainment, benefits realization, and organizational change management.

Project teams sometimes underestimate organizational change management efforts because the change seems trivial or straightforward to them when it isn't for the end-users.

Communication Is About Repetition

One summer, Yogi and Jocelyn volunteered at Heritage Park Historical Village, Canada's largest living history museum. They donned historically accurate clothing from rural Alberta's turn of the 19th century.

Heritage Park Historical Village operates a replica antique paddle steamer named the S. S. Moyie. Before guests board the steamer, they need to pick up a free ticket and walk down three long flights of rickety wooden stairs. Often, guests were unaware that a ticket was required, so they'd have to trek all the way up to the ticket booth, receive a free ticket, and then trek back down. The guests were not in a good mood after that jaunt. There were signs that a ticket was needed in many locations, but guests were often too distracted to notice.

(Continues)

(*Continued*)

> One of your authors' volunteer activities was to stand at the top of the stairs and ensure guests had claimed their tickets. We saved a lot of annoyed guests from realizing too late that a ticket was needed.
>
> It's the same with stakeholder and communication management. There can never be too much communication.

Figure 10.1 *Project communication strategies*

Is the Team Taking People Change Management Seriously?

People change management[1] is the art of successfully guiding people to change their habits and processes.

Topic	Low-risk observations	High-risk observations
People change management	The project management plan I've seen includes tasks for people change management. Related work is evident.	I haven't seen people change management referenced in the project management plan. People change management work is informal and sporadic. Related work is not evident.
PMBOK references	Sixth edition: 9.1.2.3, 9.1.3.2	Seventh edition: Figure 3-13

Low-Risk Description

The project management plan includes a plan for addressing people change management that seems reasonably comprehensive to me. Larger project teams will include a change management specialist actively executing the plan. People change management needs to consider the following:

1. How individuals will be affected positively and negatively by the change.

---

[1] People change management is also called organization change management. See the related Glossary entry.

2. How human beings respond when they fear change. If someone is worried a new process will put them out of a job, they will definitely be hostile toward it.

3. Starting at the top. Bring senior management on board first so that they, you, and the team can champion the change lower in the organization chart.

4. Communication. Your team needs to communicate a refined story that is empathic about the change's disruption and emphasizes the change's value.

High-Risk Description

The need for people change management work is a foreign concept for the more technically inclined team. High-risk people change management examples include:

1. The team actively denies the need for people change management, believing the change is trivial.

2. I've not seen any discussion about people change management in the project management plan.

3. The people change management plan I've seen is cursory or incomplete.

4. The team does not include a change management specialist, or the related tasks are not carried out.

Actions to Address High-Risk Observations

Don't kick yourself over this. People change management has been a topic of discussion for philosophers for centuries. Persuading people to change their thinking and processes is challenging. Many projects require these changes to be successful. So, you need to plan early and thoroughly to achieve the people change management you need to succeed.

Ask your project manager to walk the team through an exercise to identify where processes and people may need to change due to the implementation of the product this project is developing. Hint: If you can't come up with any changes, you aren't running a project. Projects always involve change. Ask your change management specialist to build a people change management plan to address the changes identified.

Start working with these affected departments and people early in the project. Use your political clout to communicate the importance of these changes. Leaders from the affected departments should be members of the project steering committee. Staff in these departments should receive your project communication.

Your project manager will inevitably come to you with the names of specific departments or persons pushing back hard on proposed changes. This list creates your moment as the project sponsor to shine. There is no one-size-fits-all solution for bringing the biggest naysayers around to support your project. A meeting with stakeholders to outline their concerns will be your first step. Their concerns are often about losing budget, people, and political clout. Don't mislead stakeholders about the project's intentions for your political advantage. Expect to communicate the goal and objectives of the project repeatedly. The horse and buggy industry pushed hard against the automobile industry, but eventually, the best idea won.

> The change management specialist won't be a full-time role in small and medium-sized projects. It can simply be someone tasked with performing people change management along with their other project tasks.

Is Your Data of Sufficient Quality?

Ensuring data quality[2] sufficiency is a specific Quality Assurance (QA) process where the team evaluates data accuracy and completeness.

---

[2] Data quality is included as a specific topic because almost all projects in the 21st century require data to complete successfully, even if the main product of the project is not an automated system. For example, buildings, bridges, and production facilities all depend on accurate and detailed data about facility design construction status and logistics to enable safe construction, operation, and maintenance.

Topic	Low-risk observations	High-risk observations
Data quality	I've seen a data quality evaluation plan, and it's being followed. I've observed data quality improvement work. The supporting data quality standards document looks reasonable.	I've not observed data quality evaluation work. The data quality evaluation I've observed appears rushed and uneven to meet project milestones. I've observed no data quality improvement work. The data quality standards document doesn't exist or looks incomplete.
PMBOK references	Sixth edition: No reference	Seventh edition: Figure 2-23

Low-Risk Description

The team is evaluating data quality systematically. The data quality results are readily available and shared with the QA/Quality Control (QC) team member or department so that they can monitor data quality and correction trends. The team is working with stakeholders to correct higher impact data deficiencies identified.

I feel comfortable that the data gathered relate directly to the project goal. The test data created during work on the project deliverables adequately represents the production data.

High-Risk Description

Data quality evaluation is being ignored. I don't trust the data my team presents to me. High-risk data quality evaluation examples include the following:

1. I've observed that the team evaluates data quality only when a software test fails, and the likely problem is data.
2. There is no formal documentation of what data were evaluated and what accuracy and completeness they found.
3. Some columns in the data have been evaluated, while others have not, with no indication of the reason.
4. The evaluation results are described only as a narrative with no numeric data.

Actions to Address High-Risk Observations

Your team needs to create a detailed data quality evaluation plan. This plan will include the following:

1. A list of data columns to evaluate
2. A list of software modules required to assess data quality
3. Actions to correct data inaccuracies and incompleteness
4. A list of specific stakeholders that will participate in correcting data deficiencies identified

Is There a Plan to Turn Over the Product to Operations?

The project's product will be operated somehow by an operations team for an extended period. Ensuring reasonable commissioning and the smooth start of operations requires a plan.

Topic	Low-risk observations	High-risk observations
Operations plan	I've seen an operations plan that looks reasonably complete.	I've not seen an operations plan. The operations plan that I've seen is incomplete.
PMBOK references	Sixth edition: 1.2.3.5	Seventh edition: 2.1.2, Figure 3-1

Low-Risk Description

The operations plan is reasonably complete. The team is working with stakeholders on preparations for operations.

High-Risk Description

Operations planning is being ignored. High-risk operations plan examples include the following:

1. The team has not developed an operations plan.
2. The operations plan is incomplete.
3. No one is working with stakeholders on preparations for operations.

Actions to Address High-Risk Observations

Your team needs to create a detailed operations plan. This plan will include the following:

1. Defining the deployment process. A vital feature of this process is the cutover from existing facilities and systems to new ones.
2. Defining operations processes.
3. Defining roles and responsibilities.
4. Estimating a yearly operations budget.
5. Estimating a yearly maintenance budget.
6. Hiring and training the required staff.

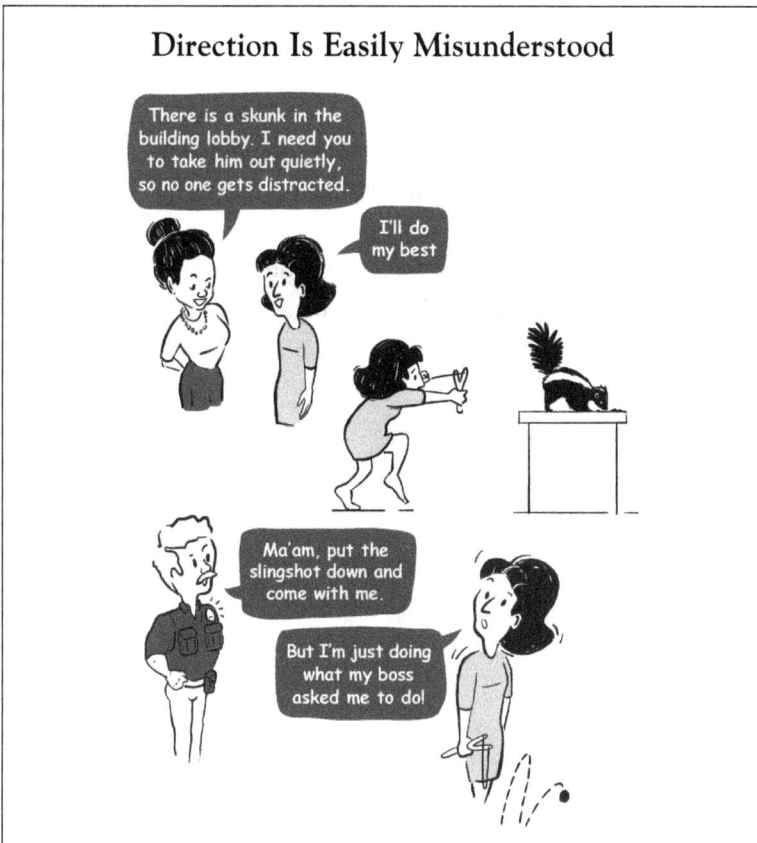

Direction Is Easily Misunderstood

(Continues)

(*Continued*)

In the comics, miscommunication, misunderstanding, and innu-endo are rampant.

In real life, all projects require a significant focus on communi-cation to:

1. Maintain a common understanding of the project goal, objectives, status, and current issues.
2. Reduce misunderstanding that will trigger rework.
3. Improve the usefulness of deliverables.
4. Improve understanding of the value of the project.

Figure 10.2 *Communicating to reduce misunderstanding*

Summary

The purpose of the deploy phase is to move the deliverables from the domain of the project team to routine use by the end-users.

The most common deploy problems include the following:

1. Rushed deployment caused by schedule pressure.
2. Slow adoption caused by insufficient organizational change manage-ment effort.

CHAPTER 11

Close

Overview

Close is the project phase that:

1. Ensures project signoff by the project sponsor and perhaps other stakeholders
2. Recognizes project achievements
3. Archives project artifacts and knowledge
4. Releases team members
5. Closes contracts

Some project teams leave too many loose ends for others to tie up in their eagerness to move on to other projects.

Specialty Cake Pans Are Fondly Remembered

Early in Jocelyn's career, she worked on a special project that entailed working past 5 p.m. most days for several months. Most team members were given a generic visa gift card as a thank-you. But Jocelyn's boss specifically gave her a gift card to the local baking supply store (Jocelyn's favorite). While the dollar amount was the same, this thoughtful gesture made Jocelyn feel like her boss knew her well and appreciated her extra effort. She still has the specialty cake pans she bought with that gift card and has made many cakes with them.

Figure 11.1 Recognizing team effort

Are You Taking Project Acceptance Seriously?

The project sponsor accepts the project as complete. This task cannot be delegated. Project acceptance is the ultimate project milestone that signifies the product can be routinely used for its intended purpose.

Topic	Low-risk observations	High-risk observations
Project acceptance	I know who is responsible for accepting the project as complete. *It's very likely you!*	I don't know who is responsible for accepting the project as complete. I can identify multiple people responsible for accepting the project as complete.
PMBOK references	Sixth edition: 5.3	Seventh edition: 2.3.5

Low-Risk Description

The project charter clearly states who is responsible for accepting the completed project. Ideally, the project charter also stipulates who is responsible for accepting milestones and deliverables. Too many cooks in the kitchen ensure that your project will never finish, and scope creep will occur. Multiple individuals could be named for large, cross-functional projects, but tread carefully. Adding more people decreases the likelihood of timely acceptance.

High-Risk Description

Multiple individuals or, worse, departments or functions are named as responsible for project acceptance. If departments such as operations, human resources or accounts payable are accountable for accepting the project, you don't know who is really in charge. If no one is specifically named, no one will feel responsible for this project, and your project will languish in a never-quite-complete state.

Another potential problem is the person named for project acceptance that is too low in the hierarchy.

Actions to Address High-Risk Observations

As you are the project sponsor, you are the person responsible for overall project acceptance. Confirm you are listed as such in the project charter.

Fight the urge to distribute this responsibility among multiple people. *You* are the best person to perform this task!

If you are a consultant, the person responsible for overall project acceptance will be someone within your client's organization.

> It can be politically tempting to declare a project success even when you know there are incomplete deliverables. This action can backfire spectacularly if the product cannot be used routinely.

While some loose ends are unavoidable, it's better to explicitly reduce scope or immediately start a successor project than risk a spectacular failure occurring just after the supposed goal line.

Are Lessons Learned Being Captured for Future Projects?

Document the positive and negative lessons you've learned during the project. The value of documented lessons learned is that they add quality, minimize rework, and reduce the risk for subsequent projects.

Topic	Low-risk observations	High-risk observations
Lessons learned	I've reviewed lessons learned being created by my team and believe they will be helpful for subsequent projects. I've reviewed lessons learned from previous projects.	I haven't seen a lessons learned register. We've faced similar issues in other projects but can't remember how they were handled or those solutions' outcomes. The lessons learned register looks incomplete.
PMBOK references	Sixth edition: 4.4.3.1	Seventh edition: 2.4.1, p. 46, 2.5.8

Low-Risk Description

There is a lessons learned register. It looks reasonably comprehensive. As the project progresses, the team updates the lessons learned register.

Example entries in a lessons learned register:

Lesson learned	Date of occurrence	Reported by	Comments
Don't work with Vendor A. They were always late.	January 7, 2020	Martina Jimenez	The team made multiple attempts to help Vendor A deliver by the date set in SOW. They did not deliver.
You will need to contact Marketing six weeks before issuing a press release.	April 12, 2020	Zuri Washington	Zuri contacted marketing two weeks before the press release was supposed to go out. She was informed their turnaround time was six weeks. She spoke with Mary Lee.
If your speakers are going to eat at the cocktail hour before the event, make sure they bring a change of clothes.	July 30, 2021	Carla Bryson	Dr. Fedorov had a colossal tomato stain on his white shirt for the duration of his talk.

High-Risk Description

High-risk lessons learned examples include the following:

1. There is no lessons learned register.
2. The lessons learned register is not up to date or easily queryable.
3. Lessons learned descriptions are too general or too high level to be helpful.
4. I know we've had similar issues in other projects, but I can't find the answers to how they were handled in the past and if those solutions were effective. So, we keep making the same mistakes over and over.

Actions to Address High-Risk Observations

Your organization may operate a knowledge management system or protocol. If so, ensure your team is aware of it and uses it for your project.

Ask your project manager to ensure the project plan includes tasks to complete lessons learned. This work is particularly beneficial at project milestones and project close.

If time permits, ask your team to think back to previous projects. If your organization doesn't operate a knowledge management system, start with a simple spreadsheet with headings that could include insertion date, project, issue description, resolution, and comments. This simple document will be better than nothing and is a way to track what you have done in the past, what worked and what didn't. When you face a similar issue in a subsequent project, you will thank your past self for taking the time to note the resolution.

Don't beat yourself up about missing lessons learned documentation. Many mature organizations and individual humans struggle with this task. You can lead by being better going forward.

Summary

The purpose of the close phase is to wrap up project work in its entirety.

The most common close problem is informal project acceptance, leading to project completion challenges.

CHAPTER 12

Conclusions

We recognize that all project sponsors are time-challenged. In response, we've:

1. Only selected the most common and potentially risky topics that projects will encounter
2. Only described immediate, tactical actions you can take to reduce project dysfunction and risk to position the project for greater success

We deliberately did not attempt an omnibus book of all or even most of the situations that projects can encounter and all the actions you might consider.

Take Action

To minimize personal risk to yourself and reduce the risk for the project, translate your vague, nagging feeling into a specific observation. We are proud of our pronounced bias for thoughtful action[1] that we've described for every potential project-killing topic in this book. We've seen too many projects fail because the project sponsor:

1. Was unsure about how to intervene in a supportive fashion
2. Hoped that a problem would work itself out or become a nonissue over time
3. Became invisible at a moment of difficulty to avoid blame and reputational damage

---

[1] See the Glossary entry for Bias for action.

As the project sponsor, if you are the source of project delay, accept or reject the recommendations expeditiously. If a stakeholder is the source of delay, it's part of your role as the project sponsor to support the project manager in pushing for a decision.

Project risks only increase through hesitation, indecision, or analysis paralysis.

Build the Project Sponsor/Project Manager Relationship

The project sponsor can build trust and appreciation for the project manager's role by reaching out proactively to build the relationship.

The project sponsor/project manager relationship is an asymmetric power relationship. The project sponsor is always more senior and has a more prominent organizational profile. On the other hand, while the project manager is less senior, they have a positive reputation for results and are seen as more technical than managerial.

The project manager is often unsure or even intimidated about the relationship with the project sponsor. However, you can strengthen the relationship because a positive, mutually supportive relationship is essential to project success.

If you've made a determined effort to build the relationship and the result is disappointing, you will have to replace the project manager. Don't drag out this decision.

For another perspective on strengthening the project sponsor/project manager relationship, please read What is a Sponsor Charter? By David Barrett, March 31, 2021.

Employ Available Resources

To build on the actions to address high-risk observations described in the book, we've created a website with additional resources that elaborate on the various topics, observations, and actions. Here's the link: www.jocelynlapointe.com/resources.

In addition, it's quick and effective to simply search for the topic that interests you.

 Celebrate successful project completions. Too often, we quickly disband the team and move on to the next urgent project or some burning crisis.

Typically, teams have worked extra hours and heroically solved long-standing problems. Project sponsors typically consider bonuses, promotions, extended paid time off, letters of commendation, and awards.

APPENDIXES

Appendix A—Role of Project Sponsors

This appendix describes what project sponsors are responsible for and how that work provides value to the project.[1] The role of project sponsors is essential and not trivial.

You can read the full Appendix at this link: www.jocelynlapointe .com/resources.

Appendix B—What Project Sponsors Don't Do

Projects are more successful when the project sponsors actively fulfill their role, as described. Because fulfilling this role is an added responsibility for most project sponsors, they do not take on additional work related to the project.[2] That's helpful for the project.

Projects experience turmoil when project sponsors engage with the project beyond their role.

You can read the full Appendix at this link: www.jocelynlapointe .com/resources.

Appendix C—Characteristics of a Successful Project Manager

This appendix describes the characteristics of successful project managers. The appendix is intended to assist project sponsors in the following:

1. Evaluating the suitability of project manager candidates
2. Guiding the discussion of their respective roles

---

[1] For more information, please read this *PMI In-Depth Report* listed in the Resources section. Executive Sponsor Engagement: Top Driver of Project and Program Success.

[2] More specifically, the project sponsor is not a member of the project team and is not assigned project tasks.

3. Collaborating with the project manager to establish their professional development plan

You can read the full Appendix at this link: www.jocelynlapointe .com/resources.

Appendix D—Value of Competent Project Management

This appendix describes the value that competent project management can bring to projects.

You can read the full Appendix at this link: www.jocelynlapointe. com/resources.

Appendix E—Phases of Projects

This appendix describes the major phases of projects. The list of phases will help you quickly confirm that your detailed project plan is reasonably complete.

You can read the full Appendix at this link: www.jocelynlapointe .com/resources.

Appendix F—Project Charter Table of Contents

This appendix contains a table of contents for project charters. You can compare this table of contents to the one in the project charter developed for your project to help you confirm that your project charter is reasonably complete.

You can read the full Appendix at this link: www.jocelynlapointe .com/resources.

Appendix G—Project Management Plan Table of Contents

This appendix contains a table of contents for a project management plan with a brief statement of the content for each item. You can compare this table of contents to the one your team has prepared to help you confirm that your project management plan is reasonably complete.

You can read the full Appendix at this link: www.jocelynlapointe .com/resources.

Appendix H—Severe Project Risk Situations

This appendix contains several lists of severe risks that will cause catastrophic project failure if one or more turn into reality. They are organized by high-level project risk categories. You can compare these severe risk statements to the contents of the risk register your team has prepared to help you confirm that your project risk register is reasonably complete.

You can read the full Appendix at this link: www.jocelynlapointe .com/resources.

Appendix I—Triple Constraint

Four Components of the Triple Constraint

Figure A I.1 The triple constraint

This appendix contains a summary discussion of the triple constraints[3] of time, scope, and cost that every project must manage to ensure project success. Because the three constraints are interdependent, projects make many tradeoffs among these constraints during the project's life. You can read the full Appendix at this link: www.jocelynlapointe .com/resources.

Appendix J—Work Breakdown Structure (WBS)

This appendix contains a summary discussion of a recommended work breakdown structure.

You can read the full Appendix at this link: www.jocelynlapointe .com/resources.

---

[3] The triple constraint is sometimes referred to as the project management triangle or the iron triangle.

Glossary

You can read the complete Glossary at this link: www.jocelynlapointe
.com/resources.

Additional References

This section contains links to publications that are helpful additional references that expand on the topics in this book.

You can read the list of resources at this link: www.jocelynlapointe .com/resources.

About the Authors

Yogi Schulz

Yogi Schulz has over 40 years of information technology (IT) consulting and project management experience in various industries. Yogi works extensively in the oil and gas industry to select and implement geotechnical, field operations, production revenue accounting, and land and contracts systems. He consults and manages projects arising from changes in business requirements, technology opportunities, and mergers. His specialties include IT strategy, data analytics, and system implementation project management. His clients have included large international organizations, midsize local organizations, regulators, and government departments.

Mr. Schulz regularly speaks to industry groups and writes a regular column for ITWorldCanada.com. He has written for *Computing Canada*, Microsoft.com, and the *Calgary Herald*. His writing focuses on project management and IT developments of interest to management. Mr. Schulz served as a member of the Board of Directors of the PPDM Association from 1994 to 2014.

Mr. Schulz holds a B. Comm. from The University of Calgary and an Information Systems Professional Certification (ISP) from Canada's Association of Information Technology Professionals (CIPS).

Yogi lives in Calgary with his wife, Connie. They have three adult children and five grandchildren.

Jocelyn Lapointe

Jocelyn Lapointe is Yogi's youngest child. After a brief career as a semi-professional opera singer, she couldn't resist the call to project management. She works as a health care project manager in Texas for a large university hospital system.

Jocelyn holds a B. Mus degree from the University of Lethbridge and a Master of Public Administration (MPA) from Brigham Young University. PMI awarded her the Project Management Professional (PMP) certificate in the Fall of 2020.

Jocelyn lives in Dallas, Texas, with her husband, Trevor, and their children, Henry and Leah.

Index

www.ingramcontent.com/pod-product-compliance
Lightning Source LLC
Chambersburg PA
CBHW061307220326
41599CB00026B/4767